John Beekman

God in creation and evolution and the church of every age in light and shade

John Beekman

God in creation and evolution and the church of every age in light and shade

ISBN/EAN: 9783337269364

Printed in Europe, USA, Canada, Australia, Japan

Cover: Foto ©Lupo / pixelio.de

More available books at **www.hansebooks.com**

AN EPIC POEM.

GOD IN CREATION AND EVOLUTION,

AND

THE CHURCH OF EVERY AGE

IN

LIGHT AND SHADE.

Non vox sed votum, non chordula musica sed cor,
Non clamans sed amans, cantat in aure Dei.
Gloss. in Cap. Cantantes.

NEW YORK:
J. S. BEEKMAN, PUBLISHER,
201-213 East Twelfth Street,
1883.

PREFACE.

AGNOSTICISM and the denial of God's agency in nature is a growing tendency of the times. The boast of scepticism is, That all things can be explained by natural laws. This arises mainly from the fact, that the earth, as a whole, is a system, an organism, and a development from one stage to a higher until Creation was finished. But in this development Spirit Power is ever manifest. The purpose for which the world and all it contains, and the heavens were made, was to reveal the glory of this Infinite Intelligence. The finishing work is Redemption and man glorified. This is exhibited on the Seventh day, not yet ended: hence no evening or morning for this day or period is mentioned in the Holy Scriptures.

To discourse upon this grand system in its order and symmetry, and show the creating, superintending, all-pervading agency of Spirit, this Spirit God, is the object of this work. Hence the author has not stopped for detail in any part, but has carried the one idea briefly through each successive stage of development. Both holy and fallen angels belong to the theme, since they are a part of creation and sustain a prominent relationship to the earth and man.

The work is an epic poem, without rhyme, as the most fitting channel to treat the great theme with brevity and force, and more especially to allow a liberty to imagination where truth is not absolutely known. Thus leading truths are given and the popular mind may receive them without the labor of hard logic.

AUTHOR.

CONTENTS.

BOOK I.

THE CREATION OF THE HEAVENS AND ANGELS.

	PAGE
Scepticism fruitless	2
God in solitude	3
Inspiration	7
Creation of matter	11
" angels	13
Satan holy	15
The angel Paradise	16
The stars formed	21
The solar planets and earth formed	25
Rest in God *because* he is infinite	29

BOOK II.

THE ANGELS' FALL.

The origin of sin	31
Sin progressive	34
Multitudes involved in Satan's fall	37
How to detect the fallen. First, by scandal	38
The same in earth	39
Second, by advocating persecution	41

	PAGE
The modern Church surpasses the worldly in this sin	42
Third, by lust of power	44
Effect of the same spirit in the Church	46
Repulsion and affinity	46
The battle in Heaven and the result	47

BOOK III.

THE CREATION OF THE EARTH.

Hell a literal place	51
The earth a solid	53
Satan instructs the fallen angels	56
Sceptics have like views	57
Evil spirits claim earth as theirs	58
Their power curtailed by the Cross alone	60

BOOK IV.

THE CREATION OF PLANTS.

What is life?	64
First plants of earth	66
The murky atmosphere	70
The fiends in it, but on the alert from fear	70

BOOK V.

A SOLAR DAY AND YEAR BEGUN.

The first day of sunshine	73
The first year	76
The starry heavens allure us to God	79
The evil spirits resume their office	81

Contents.

	PAGE
Satan calls a Council	82
His speech to render all things hurtful	84
Pastors bad and good contrasted	87

BOOK VI.
CREATION OF ANIMALS.

Enjoyment added to life	94
Fools deny God's agency	96
The waters produce abundantly	103
Coral animals produced	104
Satan rendered animals malintent	107
Satan gives death its sting	110
Devils produce imperfect taints, animosities, etc.	113
Reptiles produced	114
Gigantic fowl appear	118
Force solely originates from spirit	119
Colossal mammoths appear	120
A new race of fish and flowers appear	124
Pleasure succeeds pain as light darkness	125

BOOK VII.
CREATION OF MAN.

First a babe	127
Man's endowments	132
Eden	135
Eve created	141
The bliss of Adam and Eve while holy	143
Without Eden the powers of evil reigned as before	145
Eden a dwelling-place too for the holy angels	146

BOOK VIII.

MAN'S FALL.

	PAGE
The temptation	150
Immaterial, what form of matter spirit uses	152
Eve's fall	153
Its effect upon angels	155
Adam's fall	156
The soul increases power in sinning	159
Sentimentalism in the modern Church	161
Justice and conscience	165
Hell's jubilee over man fallen	167
Christ's descent into hell	171
Evil spirits active where good is being done	176

BOOK IX.

MAN REDEEMED.

This period divided in six distinct eras	179
The first era from Adam to the Flood	185
Adam and Eve sentenced	186
Redemption announced in Heaven	192
The summary of the whole theme stated	194
The conscience	195
The human pair driven from Eden	196
The modern Church secularized	200
The sons of Seth marrying daughters of Cain closes the first era	203
The second era begins with Noah saved	205
Ministerial success, as estimated by men, does not determine worth	205
Evil, even in the Church, should be rebuked	212
Seminaries and colleges for good or evil	216

Contents.

	PAGE
The second era ends when the Church and world amalgamated	224
The third era begins with Abraham and ends with Israel's Captivity in Egypt—the Church again absorbed by the world	225
The Church, like Lot, may be ensnared by covetousness	228
Pastors who cater to wealth	229
Pastors' vacations	231
The fourth era begins with Moses and ends with Saul made king	237
God's personal omnipresence	241
Soon death comes and then we will long for God	243
God in person near the leading feature of this era	244
Losing sight of this fact ministers preach a jargon	245
Theological seminaries	247
Ministers patronized by honorary titles	248
A place is what the spirit in it is	249
How to teach sacred truths	252
The death of Moses, and Satan claiming his body	255
The Church ought to look for sins within herself rather than and before looking without	258
The persons of the Trinity	261
Moses in person enters Heaven	264
The fifth era, monarchy	265
Begins with David	266
The clergy should introspect for sin, and not be so ready to assail others and the world	267
From suffering to glory	270
The effects of monarchy	270
David anointed king	271
Vacant churches selecting pastors	272
David loved and hated, his grace and power over men	274
David a type of Christ providing Heaven for us—Solomon's kingdom typifying the latter	277
The church in its purity	278

Contents.

	PAGE
Man nearing blissful homes	280
Solomon king and his personal excellences	281
The glory of his kingdom	282
Moloch worship permitted by Solomon	287
Church persecutions, origin and antidote	288
The world beautiful, man vile, but Heaven pure	291
Ashtareth worship also permitted by Solomon	292
The Church should rule by love	293
The sixth era, Christ born	294
The path to Heaven	296
Millennium	298
Why ungodly men are suffered to act wickedly, or are even permitted to prosper	298
Our union with God	300
The seventh era yet to come, revealed to John, of which our Sabbath is a type	301
John in Patmos was given a vision of this coming era	302
The beauty of Saints	305
Sin incidental to good	305
The possibilities of our future development	307
A glimpse of our future home	308
The exchange of this life for future felicities the price of Calvary	311

SPIRIT POWER.

BOOK I.

THE CREATION OF THE HEAVENS AND ANGELS.

AWAKE, O Muse! and sweep the sounding lyre
With skill divine, and hymn the noblest theme
Which can the mind of man or angel thrill,
Both now and evermore : awake and sing
In Heaven's harmony, of worlds evolved ;
Of plants and flowers new born ; of angel life
Began in bliss, with power to will and act ;
Of man dethroned, by sin plunged deep in hell,—
But now redeemed by God, to glory raised
High o'er the azure dome of heaven above !

Let Nature with ten thousand tongues awake
And hail the auspicious hour to sing and praise
Our Maker's grace in music of the spheres;
Let Heaven and Earth their choicest gifts employ
And chant a melody, so rich and rare,
That angels, coming near, will stay their flight
And fold their pinions, glad to tarry long!
   'Tis holy knowledge, golden fruit in rich
Abundance gives, which keeps forevermore
The wealth which neither thieves nor tyrants steal,
Which e'en in gloomy death with us abides.
Like empty, barren clouds in times of drought,
And trees uprooted, fruitless evermore
Is knowledge foolishly disclaiming God
Supreme—the Spirit Power primordial.
His presence personal pervading space
To see in every thing, is thought advanced.
For infancy, not less maturity
Of science, knowledge and intelligence,
Begin and end with Spirit Power Supreme.
Science, falsely so called, is dangerous,
Abortive and destructive otherwise.

Oh, Thou Eternal and immediate
In time, to Whom unnumbered ages gone
Or ages yet to come are moments length,
Instruct the finite mind to view Thy power
And majesty in forming act the same
Whether wrought through successive cycles past,
Beyond compute, or formed in perfect state
As soon as willed. Impressed with reverence
We'll then begin the noble, glorious theme,
A theme aglow with more than fancy's light,
Which thought in measure sweet ne'er reached before,
And feel the plenitude of infinite
Power in this richly varied universe.
To worship Thee the darkest night illumes
With rays of light which blind the commoner sense!

The Mighty God, enthroned in solitude,
The Bless*é*d, uncreated Trinity,
Fountain of good, the Godhead in repose,—
Had yet displayed no attribute of Being,
Save with the co-eternal Son and Spirit He
Abode,—one Spirit like, and each to each

Glorious, infinite, alone,—and each
To work in His own proper sphere, revealing
Perfections of the one and only God;
Nor yet had spoken either world or seraph
Into Being throughout immensity;
His beauty, grace and loveliness beyond
What creature mind has e'er conceived or known
Were yet hid in the abyss of Deity,
And all that matter and spirit life reveal
Known only to Himself, God infinite!
In solitude—a dreadful Deity!
Our spirit faints beneath the awful thought,
Too ponderous for human, finite strength!
His realm was infinity, with nought
Else but pure spirit, personal, enthroned
In light ineffable and glorious.
For in the ether blue no star in light
Of amber shone and twinkled 'mid the gloom;
No creature having life adored the throne,
Nor ranged joyously through the heavenly realms;
Nor was there tree or flower, beast or bird
Yet born to render nature beautiful,—

But God alone, in thought inscrutable,
Profound, possessed of possibilities
Beyond what Heaven yet knows in solitude!
No marvel hence that graciously He pleased
To break eternal silence and reveal
Himself in worlds, and other spirit life;
To share with myriads bliss ineffable;
And hence to will and cast a universe
And mould it into being, in which to act
Himself, best illustrated, but far short
Of all the vast and awful truth involved,
By human soul within controlling body,—
Within and yet above whate'er's controlled!

    Oh God, too good Thou art to keep unshared
Thy goodness and too great to live alone!
Beyond, in timeless past, when time and space
Were not, Thy light, O, dreadful thought! alone
Did shine,—immensity alone Thy throne!
As Son and Holy Ghost, co-equal dwelt
Ever with Thee in bliss ineffable,
So in Thy bosom sweetly nurtured may
We rest, and nestle folded in Thy arms

Live always in Thy Person dread but dear,
And thrilled with ecstacy and love enjoy
Thy gorgeous face in beauty and caress!
We tremble at the near approach we make
To Thee—at our request so seeming bold!
Our sight will dazzle by Eternal rays
Which in Thy Person shine,—and yet we come
O God! to Thee,—to perish in Thy arms
Content if needful, ravished by Thy love!
But vain it is to tremble or to fear,
For tenderness and love forever beam
From Thy sweet face—more readily Thou seekest
Us than we seek Thee,—only seemingly
Thou art remote—nor wilt repel our love.
Thou'rt hidden now in part to be revealed
More fully upon the hills of Paradise,
Where better we shall love and bear Thy light!
Oh Fountain inexhaustible, we drink
In Ocean's bliss in seeing, loving Thee!

Come! pilgrim through the vale of life with me,
From life to death upon the shores of time—

Creation of the Heavens and Angels.

From death to life upon the shores of bliss,
Come, learn with me the mystery of Heaven—
Within the soul, of happiness complete,
Of spirit power divine in gorgeous light.
We'll tarry in the shades of night at times
The better to discern the pure and true :
We'll traverse plains and heights ne'er reached before,
Be dazzled too, at times, by rays divine,
And views obtain appalling human sense :
Into the depths we'll revel seeking God—
But ever is He near and manifest,
And in the end reach home—Elysian fields !
  Prophets are given of God, and solely, vision
Of past or prophecy of things to come—
Eyes spiritual, vision answering
To bodily, from time and sense divorced,—
Now Heavenly and divine, the Vision God's :
As instinct exercised unerringly
Is Wisdom God's, whereby the brutes surpass
And shame and put to blush the powers of man.
'Tis not of man or angel, creature born,
To look into the dark profound of ages

Since, ere he came to Being or the earth
Or Heavens were lighted in the firmament;
Nor into future times, as yet unborn—
Against our nature and beyond our powers.
God moves with Hand Divine the mists away,
Throws light upon a scene—and tells us look!—
Behold! through Spirit Infinite we see—
Through eyes Divine: and Vision God's a scene
Impresses upon our souls, infallible
Then and alone, thus helped by Spirit Power
Above, outside ourselves and infinite!
'Tis Blessed Spirit here, companionating
With finite in gracious intimacy—
Heaven's Wisdom, Glory, Love or Power disclosed
Long since or yet reserved, revealed to earth
And man, or angels in empyrean heights!
To say we're helped, as helmsmen are to guide
A bark unerringly o'er stormy seas,
Are supervised to keep from error free—
Called Inspiration, given of God to men
Who wrote the Sacred Word, is short of truth,
Or stated but in part by half at least!—

The word is good and orthodox, retained—
But as interpreted as well expunged :
Called Supervision would disclose the view
As taken and clear of all entanglements.
But there's a vision given above our powers
Of brilliant gems upon the ocean's bed
And golden palaces with crystal halls,
Of hidden rocks and shoals, blind rocks and shoals
Beneath dark inky waves ; there is a Hand
Removing shades, imposing light, and God
Is eye who casts a vision upon the soul,
The spirit born, finite and limited.
Thus more than helped, or merely supervised,—
God's Vision, infallible, an image casts
Within our soul, and spirit sees the truth,
To speak or write, unerringly, each word,
As given original, by Power Divine.
We're helped as human eyes are instruments
Of spirit : thus is God pre-requisite,
And not a mere adjunct or accident !
Thus only man the future or the past
Discerns, as Moses, prophet of the Lord

Discerned Beginning of the Universe,
Angels as yet unborn, and through all time
Into the abyss and shades of night delved deep
And saw the past and future's history.

    As human eyes perceive a flower and know
The fact, requiring evidence no further,
And laughs to scorn a sceptic asking proof
And further demonstration of the fact,
So God's Vision, imparting truth for thought,
Pleasure and help throughout life's pilgrimage
To spirits born, impressing scenes beyond
What mortals otherwise could know, cries halt!—
To every doubt and sceptic scheme which steals
A march within the lines of truth's strong citadels!
When souls discern through Vision God's, the past
Or future mysteries, 'tis gross to cavil,—
For further evidence none need to ask.

    To Heaven! let earth's incense most sweet ascend
For Inspiration given to sinful man;
For mysteries disclosed and treasuries
Unsealed where richest gems with lustre glow!

Creation of the Heavens and Angels.

O! fellow pilgrim, mark the birth of dust
Whence stars were made, and man and angel form,
And marvelling adore the first display
Of Power Divine—Almighty God revealed!
Born by the word omnific God declared
There sprang a universe, a gaseous realm
Of matter into Being, rarified
Like air from centre to circumference.
Whence issued suns in multitude like pearls
And crystal sands which deck the ocean's floor,
Whose heat and brightness far exceed our own,
And all the worlds which plough the ether main.
Whate'er material is, from gaseous state
Arose, and into its original
Returns when it its destiny fulfils.
Combined harmoniously are clustered suns,
The system one, where peace and happiness
Have held their reign supremely sweet since first
It rolled a formless airy mass in space:
And wondrous suns which gyre around and round,
As if in passionate pursuit, with joy
Each eyeing the other's changing beauty's hue:

And glimmering clouds of worlds o'er many a rood
So far and wide a shooting beam of light
E'en tires on wing ere it their limits gains.
    The worlds, suns, systems filling space evolved,
Moulded by hand divine all beautiful,
From elements, the dust original,—
As rude and blackened coal when pierced by heaven's
Lustre becomes a diamond bright and chaste;
Or like as crystalline formed from the crude
And shapeless dust of earth. Here then we look
As upon a forest growth in every stage
Of germs developed from the tiny sprout
Just peeping out the soil its tender head
To the exalted tree that rears its trunk
Against the sky and proudly spreads its boughs
Of perfect beauty which reflect the light.
The elements original of matter
Are few—or possibly there's only one—
But O! how endless the variety
Of body and of substance they assume,
And marvellous their beauty to attract
The eye, or ugliness repelling thought:

As flesh of gases elementary
Is formed the same and like in animal kind :—
But mark the maiden, fair and sweet, compared
With serpent flesh, repulsive, hard and cold !
So diamond beautiful and lustrous
Is carbon, and an elementary
Gas, and likewise coal which is lustreless.
So bodies there are, tenements of spirit,
Celestial and terrestrial, whether seen
Or not by us, alike composed of substance
According to their kind and sphere and realm,
Of matter simple and original,
Born by omnific word, the Spirit Power
Who was ere man or angel breathed, the light
That solely shone throughout immensity !

    O, pilgrim in the shades of solitude,
Reclused from things of sense and time, Behold !
An order of Creation in advance
Of matter far and incomparable
Now appear,—finite spirit,—angel life,—
Intelligences pure and holy, like

To God, with thought and sentiment and heart
And faculties and conscious will endowed;
And tenements superadded to spirit,
Called bodies, like pure ether, richly formed
Of elements from which the universe
Is made,—an airy substance, not discerned
By carnal sense, save otherwise they will
To manifest themselves in earth or heaven.
So animalculæ, perceptible
To none, are yet organic substances
With functions requisite to life and pleasure.
For bodies are adapted to the sphere
In which each spirit acts, expands and thinks.
Whether the tenements of soul are formed
In solids, flesh and bone, or gaseous, like
Thin air, but having beauty, shape and form
Discerned by angel spirits and our souls
When disembodied, is quite immaterial.
Our bodies earthy take the form of earth;
But angel bodies heavenly in form,
A light and gaseous substance like to Heaven.
The great Apostle of the Gentiles hence

Denominates the mass of men as fools,—
Because, forsooth, they foolishly inquire
Respecting resurrection—with what bodies
Do they come ? seemingly a question great,
Important—really immaterial.
To culture soul, and to prepare for high
And spiritual work should be the end
Of body, whether gaseous or in flesh.

 Then Satan, towering pre-eminent
O'er all the myriads which there into Being
Came, was archangel 'mong the mighty hosts,—
With attributes and powers transcendent,—fresh
In youth and beauty as the morning light,—
With intellectual faculties ne'er since
Surpassed,—with dignity befitting him,
Having no peer around the throne of God ;
Whose character was lovely and adorned
With virtue, as a halo of pure light
Illumes a person unalloyed with sin ;
His body of so fine a mould it shone
In air or ether or at heaven's throne
Like to a transparent luminary,

But yet organic, linking him to matter
And spirit, substance having suitable
To his employments, nature and desire
To range the universe of God's domain.
His honored name by which while pure and holy
He was known, is forgotten since his fall!

    For Satan and the countless angels great
Or small, all holy in ecstatic bliss,
A lofty habitation God prepared,
Adapted to their nature, labors, tastes
And all acquirements destined to engage
Their powers superior eternally.
From centre to circumference entire,
The universe of matter was one Globe,
An elemental mass unformed as yet
In either suns or worlds,—a chaos crude
And marvellously dark,—a wonderful
Expanse whose limits e'en an angel swift
As light for centuries could scarcely reach :
Where now glow worlds upon worlds, suns and stars
Illuminating heaven's vast expanse.
The angels' Eden was the centre, whence

Every way they could view alike the works
Of God, no east or west or north or south,—
Alike above, below, to right or left,
So that where'er they looked a wonderful
Display of Spirit Power was manifest.
Here was prepared an angel Paradise.

    Like phosphorescent light upon a sea
Which storms have broken into million caps
Of foam and spray, now calm, the gale allayed;
So God's command illumed the angel world,
And carefully the cradle of their birth,
The home of their maturity adorned.
Darkness now ceased to reign! with light the first
Created power, the fountain head of all
The streams of life was ended first of days.
From centre to circumference light shot
Darting throughout the elements like tongues
Of flame: the dazzled universe was thrilled!
Thus northern lights illume the firmament
When winter has thick ribbed the earth with ice,
And while the sun's benign rays are withheld.
The angels now in wonder rapt, amazed

Beheld themselves, their forms, alike illumed,—
The beauty of the heavens theirs concrete,—
Their bodies shedding color, lustre, hue
And shade such as adorned the heavenly realms.
Whichever way they looked some new display
Dazzled their senses and restrained their breath,
Inured not yet to glory now revealed.
This heaven, centre of the mighty Globe,
Was like a molten sea of glittering gems :
Where districts seemed of massive silver, bright
But mellow brilliants, others yellow gold,
With varied tints like clouds at setting sun.
Heaven aflame with more than rainbow hues
Scattered her myriad diamonds, emeralds
And every precious gem like autumn leaves,
To light and beautify her mighty realm.
For beauty, pleasure and utility
Nature has possibilities unthought
Or dreamed,—as dark seeds open into flowers,
And tiny acorns into monarch oaks,
And pearly shell removed an eagle mounts
Above storm-clouds and soars imperial,

And gorgeous butterflies from worms adorn
The earth and air and range from flower to flower.
 The legions of pure angels soon became
Enamored with their home. And every new
Display of beauty, power, intelligence
Enrapt their thought and formed a fitting theme
For social converse sweet, which never soured
Their appetite or tired their intercourse.
Here spirit finite shared the joy and bliss
Of Deity, and were employed in all
That elevates and renders soul ecstatic,—
Shedding the light of Spirit Infinite.
How beautiful, how bright the angels were—
How blessed to share the bliss of Deity!
 The elements primordial, the Globe
Of matter, ever in its gaseous state
Might have remained except for Spirit Power.
For solids by laws natural return
Into their elements original,
When they've fulfilled their office, once ordained.
The archangels noting some great change near,
Thereupon held converse apart and deemed

It prudent to assemble every angel
Within their heavenly precincts secure.
The myriads were scattered everywhere:
In fields of oxygen a multitude
Discoursed upon its affinity in less
Or great proportion with the gases,
Which they from near or from distant fields brought;
Illuminating parts with phosphorous,
With sulphur others into splendor such
As mortal eye or sense could not endure:
Some in districts of Hydrogen, or Carbon,
Or other elements all pleasurably
Employed. Some journeyed upon the points of light,
The darting beams, to reach the bounds of space.
Some gathered gems, both diamonds, emeralds,
Rubies from fields where beauty glowed intense.
Nature was lavish now of beauty only!
Far in the sphere of heaven's universe,
The marvellous dome all around from where
He stood, a trumpet voice in thunder tones
Was heard, which echoed and re-echoed till
Every angel stood mute and motionless.

'Twas Satan calling them and anxiously
To annul the intervening space between
Them and him in their quick returning flight !
None questioned—all obeyed—no time was lost !
Their pinions cleaving elemental air
Like arrows from a bow, an army dense,
A tempest raised, such as excite the ocean
When whirlwinds sweep through her utmost depths.

    Their speed was timely. Moanings deep and dire,
And thunderings throughout the gaseous Globe
Gave evidence of some new wonder near.
Already heaven's centre separate
Became, and other globes of million leagues
Twice told diameter of liquid fire,
And millions,—all like evenly balanced,—hung
'Pon nothing,—mutually co-acting,—self-poised ;—
And vast and deep the mighty chasm between—
An empty space and void which we call ether.
For 'twas God's voice that thundered, Spirit Power,
Who in the majesty of might appeared
And said, Be there a firmament between
The waters and let it divide the waters

From the waters ! And God made the firmament,
The ether's wide expanse, transparent blue,
Dividing chaos elementary
Above, beneath : the firmament called heaven.

    Pilgrim of earth and time from lofty heights
We've retrospected ancient night, ere light
Appeared, and have conceived that matter void,
Inert was spread about the central power,
When into systems formed, they all revolve.
E'en though untrue in each particular,
Conceit o'erdrawn, a vision limited
And circumscribed, 'tis yet a pleasing thought
And may be true, conceived as probable.
From out infinity's waste Spirit Power
Thence called them forth to life. Before there reigned
A solitude akin to Egypt's night,
A death we'd shun above what reigns in tombs !
No music of the spheres, now full of life,
No ether wave to lash the worlds as water
A vessel ploughing ocean's mighty main.
Not thus forever could the universe

Remain, for power filling immensity
Was felt to energize with quickening life.
As parent bird the glow of life imparts,
So God's breath moved upon the water's surface
From which the universe evolved,—the pulse
Of life then throbbed throughout chaotic void,—
Impelled by Spirit Power the atoms moved
And systems formed about the central Power,
Which light and beautify the firmament:
Centaur, and Cygnus robed in lilac blue,
And brilliant Sirius, and all that shine,
In anthems sing the music of the spheres,
The solar too whence earth and planets grew.

    The immensity of power and harmony,
Number and beauty of celestial worlds
As suns, astonish the wise of every age.
The mighty suns, the clusters; double worlds •
Of light, and nebulæ as islands vast
Are seen to float upon an ocean's depth,
Whose limits thought can scarcely reach, whose height,
Whose abyss is beyond—and deeper still
Though we descend eternally their depths

With finite powers excursive in their range.
Here calmly undisturbed by storms they shine
More beauteous than the flowers of joyous spring,
Or tinted leaves of autumn's long decline.
A lustre of their own they shed as gems
Of earth, but varied more in brightened hues.
Andromeda appears as robed in green
Like earth, and Argus flashing yellow flames
As topaz, for which misers barter Heaven;
And some of amethyst, a purple tinge
As clouds of evening when the sun has set.
Some shine a sapphire of cerulean hue,
Others in ruby's red, some in the mild
And chastened glow of diamonds polished bright.
    O, wonderful the omnipotence divine
Which throughout space directs in harmony
Vast myriads of creature worlds and keeps
Their massive globes from dashing one against
Another, whose confusion then would drive
The ether waves with heinous booming shrieks
Into the very gates of hell to arouse
The reigning powers of death and set them free!

Creation of the Heavens and Angels.

These myriad suns and archipelago
Of suns controlling vassal spheres unseen,
Planets and worlds of systems complicate
Move in a circling orbit, as the earth
About the sun, around one central power.
O! where does the eternal Majesty
Reside round which our system, sun and worlds,
Revolves with giddy speed, which is in bonds
As are the solar worlds joined close to all
The clusters vast of creature stars and systems
In heaven's dome, which nightly shed their rays?
God sways His potent sceptre through this space
Powdered with myriad systems densely strewn!

Pilgrim, we've ranged in quick excursive flight
The universe, the heavens and angel homes,
And limit now our vision and our thought
To earth and solar planets, glad to see
Them into Being come, all orderly,
Governed by laws ordained eternally.
As Solar from the universal Globe,
One sole united mass, was rent and torn,

So Neptune separate became and moved
Within its orbit, and Uranus next
Her train six satellites, then Saturn bright
With moons and arch of heaven's pure lustre formed
As if designed to welcome spirits blessed,
And dreary Jupiter and glowing Mars.
All these as watchful sentinels parade
In ceaseless march beyond our little orb, .
Which like them was delivered from the same
Chaotic womb. Within our globe's embrace
Fair Venus grew in chastened modesty,
And now in twinkling beauty shines the queen
Of all the starry hosts,—first heralding
The early morn, and in the dusky eve
Glances one charming look upon the earth
And disappears. Thus the fair eastern nymph
Unveils her face to our enchanted gaze,
Then playful hides her charms and glides away.
And last of all the sun's bright retinue,
Almost hid by the splendor of her beams,
Was Mercury formed into globe opaque.
  These all attend upon her Majesty,

The attractive power that keeps in harmony
Their orbs as subjects to her ruling sway.
Thus as a mighty screen the firmament
Divided the waters and formed heaven's vault.
Thus closed the morning of the second day.

    The tuneful planets roll with music sweet,
Singing,—Almighty God, eternal King,
Thou'rt holy, holy, holy evermore!—
With thrilling voice they hymn creative praise—
The choirs like cherubim with harps of gold
To which the angels listen, and God, well pleased,
Delights to hear—His works attuned to song!

    Tired pilgrim! we'll here retrospect the road
We've travelled o'er, and rest our weary feet,—
Having seen power omnipotent displayed,
Which won from formless chaos, first of things,
Our solar sphere,—and how displayed conceived:—
The moon a formless waste once round the earth,
With it the earth and planets round the sun,
The solar with the other systems one
Globe entire, undivided mass. When broken

And separate into spheres, systems, suns,
Then all revolved each one as now around
A central power, joined by all the other suns
And worlds unseen throughout the universe :—
All wheels, within a wheel of dreadful height,
Whose vast circumference is far as space
Is found and resting upon shores infinite,
And full of eyes,—the Spirit Power, Supreme,
And finite power, for spirit is the eye :—
All which Ezekiel, seer divine, perceived,—
A vision of the universe and earth
And Heaven, and God enthroned Supreme o'er all !

    Earth is an organism ; our solar sphere
Likewise ; and so the universe with each
And all systems, stars and suns and worlds ;
Governed in whole by simple laws,—none greater
Than are repulsion and affinity.
So are great truths surprisingly most simple,
While error is complex, confusing thought !

    'Tis foolish to ignore a pilot hand
To guide the helm of worlds and suns and systems
Through ether's wide expanse immeasurable !

With fear and reverence we may indulge
The happy thought, that all these glorious stars,
Together with the suns now beauteous,
Roll round the throne of heaven's Almighty King,—
The place robed in light incomparable!

   Thus far has Spirit Power in light alone
Been seen, revealed in beauty and in might.
Oh, Greatness infinite! there's room for all
That is in Thee—and yet the universe
A very little thing exists,—compared,
A mote that glitters in the light, a leaf
That floats upon the ocean's bosom vast:
Yet less than infinite, less great and high,
Thou'd crush our fragile powers, our feeble sense!
In Thee is home, a shelter for the soul,
Because Thou'rt Infinite, and Great, and Good,
Where poorest mortals struggling find their rest
Amid the strifes of life—in Thee alone!
In Thee, no sense or fear of rivalry
Will quench our ardor, love or reverence!
In thee, we share a part of infinite,

A part of glory which pertains to Thee,
Of beauty and of grandeur filling heaven,—
Advance and glory in Thy might, which ne'er
We'll reach or rival, but will always love !
Upon a boundless bosom we're sustained
In Thee, and everywhere and place is home !—
From Thee, we ne'er can drift or hide ourselves.
O ! Grandeur rendering us grand ; and Wealth
That makes us rich ; and Goodness that makes good,
Within Thy light communicate to us
While resting in the bosom of Thy love !—
And cradled there we'll rest, nor dream of harm.

BOOK II.

THE ANGELS' FALL.

As God the parents of our race instructed
To dress and keep and render beautiful
Paradise, so angel powers were employed
To render heaven redolent with sweets,—
With wealth the rarest universe could furnish,—
With glory ravishing to every soul.
'Twas spirit finite power in exercise.
Peerless was Satan, intellect profound,
Who shone among the countless legions fair
As though he were Supreme—a very God.
Clearly whatever was within the reach
Of finite powers he saw with accuracy,
As though all eyes or ears or intellect.
An alchemist profound, constructing gold

And every precious metal to adorn
The place of his abode, and precious gems
From elements whence worlds and suns are made,—
An ocean's wealth within his easy reach.
The universe was levied upon to yield
Her choicest treasure heaven to beautify.
Each angel praised the Prince, and multitudes
Adoring prostrate at his feet revered
Their chief—to worship and sin near allied !
Worship and sin is always near akin !
    Satan now thought upon Himself—reflex
Of sin, and gave not God all praise,—declined
Not to receive a form of worship heaven
Forbids to any save to God Supreme.
The angel which to John in Patmos came
Declined such honor from the agéd seer,—
Saying, See thou do it not—worship God !
Doubtless 'twas love and reverence in John,
A sense of gratitude and love which moved
His quick obeisance at the angel's feet,
His head bowed low : but 'twas a form of sin
About to be conceived in embryo,

Deceptive and like to mislead the heart
Both of the worshipper and worshipped, man
And angel : hence quickly he was rebuked.
'Twould have been sin conceived in worshipper
And worshipped, in effect a prodigy
Of ill full born, had not the angel checked
The tendency seen in the prophet's heart :—
In angel for receiving, in the seer
For giving what to God alone belongs.
Thus sin originates in misdirected
Worship, where God is quenched in self or others.
Hence solemnly God warns,—" Quench not the Spirit ! "
The angel's name is not revealed, but doubtless
'Twas Gabriel, who ever bore good news
To men. He lovely in attire and mien,
Holy and wise, would not fail to recall
The like temptation Satan failed to endure
In Heaven, by angels loved, revered and served !
Thus daily, men accounted righteous, sin,
Reflecting upon themselves,—and homage due
To God alone receiving gratefully
And with delight ;—both looking for and lusting

After man's praise, instead of being zealous
For God.   And clergymen at altars holy
Are first to sin in this particular,
As Satan was, archangel once in heaven!
　　Sin is progressive, scarcely recognized
As sin at first, like germs whence reptiles spring.
Sin born in thought of self, with subtlety
Waxed strong in Satan, and sad havoc made!
His own sublimity he now admired;
Was zealous for self-honor; and conceit
Quenched thought of God, and all dependency
Upon a Higher Power, subordinate.
Inflated now with pride, he fell—and great
His fall! Heaven seemed a chamber charged with death!
'Twas like a cloud obscuring Heaven's light,
The first of such the universe had seen.
Clouds intervene to hide the sun's bright rays,
But still the sun beyond, above, is just
As bright and beautiful and pure in light.
So sin is moral shade, and densely dark
At times, obscuring heaven's glorious rays,
But uncorrupted thereby is God's light

And blissful purity, immaculate.
Now sin casts heavy clouds upon the world
Of spirits—realms of bliss whose light's obscured !
Grandeur magnificent defouled and fallen !
'Twas new, and born of finite spirit power
Acted upon and acting selfishly.
So even if insects or birds or beasts
Are purely selfish, they impair instinct,
And compass their own death, not long delayed.
Danger is always near if acts are done,
Or thoughts conceived without there's God in them,
For either man or angel, insect, beast,
Or any creature having finite spirit.
For instinct even is God's wisdom solely,
To govern creature kind unerringly.
Earth's greatest Teacher, Christ divine from Heaven,
His followers forewarned, Beware of men :
And when betrayed, for their defence to take
No thought,—since God through and in them would
    speak.
Hence acting independently of God,
Ignoring spirit Power Supreme, unmoors

The soul from her sure anchorage, unbars
The gates of evil passions, pride and lust,—
And finite spirit will most surely fall,
Acting against herself and nature's God,
And journey on the highway paved for hell,—
Like worlds adrift without an end or aim
Unmoored from genial power to guide their course,
Or with'ring flowers deprived of Parent Sun—
Save that these die and must dissolve, but soul
Increases power by that upon which it feeds
For either good or evil, pain or pleasure.
Hence Babylon's profane and haughty king
In pride of heart exulting said, To heaven
I'll ascend, and my throne exalt above
The stars of God, in heights above the clouds:
For is not this great Babylon which I
Have built? The word had scarcely passed his lips
Ere thunderbolts from heaven struck down the Prince,
Son of the morning, and like Lucifer
He fell, and lost his kingdom and his pride.
So too a miserable King of Tyre,
Spoken of in Ezekiel's prophecy,

Brought shame, dishonor, ruin upon himself,
And lost his pleasure in a paradise
Of sweets, his beauty too like morning mists.
Scripture makes each a type of Satan fallen
Through pride and self-conceit from heaven and glory.

    A multitude of angels vast and dense
In Satan's snare were taken, and began
Their fall in creature admiration, since
Prolific in a progeny of devils
Among the human kind. 'Twas not a sin
To admire a creature, but unguarded led
Thereto ; a rose which had a thorn concealed.
In knowledge, power and splendor all excelled ;
In happiness and honor unsurpassed ;
In virtue, favor with God, dignity
Unrivalled,—yet rebelling they sank deep
Into the depths of shame and misery,—
Incurred contempt of all the holy angels,
And endless wrath of Heaven and God Supreme !
Against a most beneficent Creator
And Sovereign they wickedly rebelled.
Except obedience to natural

Laws, regulating purity of life,
They unrestrained were,—no restraint was felt.
'Twas hard for holy angels to detect
At times the lapsed, for lineaments of light
And purity long with the lost remained;
And God for wise ends, known best to Himself,
Suffered a war long and continuous
Between the evil angels and the good,
Akin to what is re-enacted here.
Archangel Michael led heaven's hierarchies,
And Satan marshalled heaven's malcontents,
Each watchful to discriminate between
Their friends or foes, the righteous and the wicked.

    Evil reports were rife in heaven now.
The sinning angels anxiously gave willing
Ear to their fellows who had hurtful tales
To tell, and gave them wing, and circulated
Bad news and gossip, stopping not to inquire
The truth,—their tongues aflame with evil speech:
Angels among the worst, to mischief given.
Such patronize and pity and condole
While secretly they say hard things,—and feign

The Angels' Fall.

Sorrow for victims whom they victimize!
This fixed their place as scavengers in Satan's
Armies; cowards who follow in the wake;
Like graveyard Ghouls which feed upon putrid flesh,—
Of Satan even judged of little worth!

    Alas! that men should act the same at times,
As terriers on scent to catch a hare,
Whose business 'tis to watch their Master's house.
Corrupted, such do lack the charity
That sweetens life, are cruel 'gainst their kind
With no purpose to help themselves thereby,
But simply sport in ills and strifes produced—
Hardhearted, feasting upon the pains of others!
There's one apology in their behalf
Which charity bids speak with bated breath,—
That Nature's been too sparing of her gifts
Perhaps, and thus incompetent for good
They range and hunt and hound and rend alone!
If each would probe his heart himself he'd find
The worst of men—a Devil in disguise—
Save for the grace of God, and arms Divine

About him thrown in love—love marvellous!
The light which renders clear to self self-guilt
And shame, obscures or hides the faults of others.
Then other men seem great, ourselves but mean;
Others good, but ourselves too vile to live;
Others noble, but ourselves base, ill born;
Others righteous, but ourselves a sepulture
Whited without but full of dead men's bones.
Heaven's light will blind the eyes to others' faults,
Hell's darkness quicken sight to all but self!
Dark are the souls which flit from flower to flower
And cull but poison, where honey too abides!—
Which only scent the rank and fetid air,
Where much of sweetness too predominates!
Man's image photographs itself as good
Or vile, and paints from self the evils talked
To prejudice or do a harm to others!
In others innocent, adulterers
Will see self-guilt conceived or done!
Hence talk and scandal best betray a guilt
At home, within the scavengers themselves.
The ways of God obscure or bury faults,—

Which men unearth to shame their kind—themselves !
Each soul should be an orb of light, attracting,
Alluring other souls, imparting light
Alone to each, like suns in ether pure—
Be Heaven, bestowing beauty, grace and love
Upon other spirits favored less, as worlds
About the sun, each having excellence
Which none but God, their Maker, fully knows !
How sweet to dwell within the light of souls
Most pure and drink the nectar they distil !
'Tis Heaven below and we in love with Heaven !

    Apollyon advocated zealously
To roast with fire all heretics, or such
As differed from him in views entertained—
An appetizer to a hungry maw ;
A fierce spirit, who feigned a zeal for God,
And advocated learnedly with power
To expel from the army militant
There, every angel not employed as he
And Michael were, though such might ardently
Desire to battle for the Lord's elect

In mean and humble stations when their chief's
Will should be indicated,—humble angels,—
Misfortune and sin lying at others' door their crime!
Thus Michael saw in him and others like
In views, his foes in heaven's livery.

    Thus many in the earth and in the church
Religion from e'en equity divorce,—
Or yoked with sin in hell's triumphal car
Adopt and advocate views, and crimes commit
'Gainst e'en morality. Hence history,
Alas! records against the church deeds done
By ministers in priestly robes adorned
So horrible, cold, cruel, that the heart
Of even wicked men disgusted turns
With sickened pallor from the horrid sight.
For purity when prostituted sinks
Into vile depths proportioned by the heights
Whence fallen, as virgins sweet become the worst
Abjects, outcasts and blind to shame when lost,
And readily will perpetrate a crime
Without a blush which hardened men will shun!

Cruelly keen are shafts, and poisoned too,
The clergy use when they begin attack
Without divine authority, beneath
Their office, 'gainst another of their order,—
More dangerous become than wicked men,
In using Heaven's artillery against
The saints, a war in Heaven's sacred place!
Religion is not justly charged therewith,
But lack of it, perversity of heart.
'Tis Satan clothed in heaven's vestments pure
And clean, and these the eye of sense discerns.
Alas! the deeds disrobe an ugly devil!
But superficial thinkers hence infer
That Scripture faith and all religions are
Inimical, unfriendly to the race,
And scoff, blaspheme and rail against the church,
Whose virgin purity by sin is soiled—
The sin their kind entail and propagate,
Appearing like dead flies in ointment pure,
Where best its rankest scent may be discerned.
Their sins in ministers, where purity
Is claimed and hoped for by e'en worldly men,

Are ranker than the flames of sulph'rous hell,
And smell to the utmost verge of heaven's vault—
There most confound and shame the profligate!
No wonder hence they howl against the church
Combined, without discriminating good
And bad, and all religion in the world,
When ministers lapsed best condemn their crimes,
And tortured leer and whine for very pain!
If all the race were like involved in ruin,
One common hell, and none were true and pure,
They'd shout and dance Satanic jubilees!

 While war progressed in Heaven and sides were taken
Azrael assumed pre-eminence above
The rest, disputed with Michael the right
Of leadership, and thought himself the best
Fitted by far to conquer and subdue
The enemy. His sacrilegious claims
And bold effrontery resisted, sharp
Practices subtly were then devised,
And agents predisposed unto deceit

Most actively obeyed their petty chief
And raised the standard of a new revolt,
A sub-rebellion 'mong the holy angels.
One Israfil his master's trumpet blew
Loud and strong, obedient to any work
Imposed—a servile, dirty, cringing slave,
Became a herald zealous to create
Alarm and raise a tumult, planned in secret.
Satan, pleased, took no part in such revolts:
No need: such agents do effective work,
Resembling closely their great prototype.
Without delay or parley such were driven
Among the enemy, eternally,
(For Michael and his helpers were above
The servile fear for discipline in Heaven,)
Their character revealed—and self-deceived
They seemed to wonder why heaven's wrath was
    kindled
Against them so innocent and devout!
'Twas thus with Korah's company, who strove
With Moses, lusting for the leadership,
Whom quickly yawning earth's abyss devoured.

'Tis thus with churches often in the world,
Too commonly, alas ! in modern times,
Whose condemnation cannot slumber long,
Though mercy lingereth and God forbears
To execute His wrath upon such sin
Forewarned in Dathan and Abiram's fate,
Who famous were in the great congregation.
Any who lust for office in the church
Endanger and defile the beautiful
Zion, akin to Heaven, which God has loved
And founded for the saving of our race,
And prove a carnal heart and moral death—
For even membership unfit—debarred
By lust of power,—the origin of sin !
None save the meek, devout and lovable,
Who shrink from having power, should office hold.
Shocking for man to lord God's heritage,
Which done will always blight and shame the church.
Where Satan works let pastors guard with care !

Repulsion and affinity prevail
Through nature's wide domain : so morally

And socially one creature to another
Is drawn or otherwise repelled without
Knowing or caring for the reason why.
A sinner is repelled by holiness,
The righteous an affinity for each
Other have, both here and eternally.
Sin having entered heaven, unholy angels
Felt a repulsion from the holy ones,
And *vice versâ;* but each class were closer
Drawn by an influence whose force they never
Hitherto had experienced, binding them
As one in unity and interest,—
The first beneficent effect of sin
Having entered Heaven's sacred precincts—
A light which shines intensely 'mid the gloom,
Rendering bliss more blissful e'en in Heaven!

 A perfect sifting having been secured,
Michael in solid phalanx marched against
Satan, alike prepared, his marshalled hosts
Of myriads drawn up, arrayed for battle,
Who fiercely frowned, malignant, upon his foe.
Heaven quaked from centre to circumference!

'Twas finite spirit power in close conflict,
Which earth reveals in every phase of life,
And seen in all society, among
The rich and poor, the wise and ignorant
Alike, in every place about the globe
Wherever man sojourns, to bless or curse
His home, conditioned upon the spirit nourished;
Where evil is opposed to good, and good
To evil; sinners are arrayed, malign,
In hell's panoply to subvert the good,
And saints in heaven's vestments to subdue
The bad and bring the reign of glory back
Again,—in love for all the race and world—
Divine their spirit, near akin to God.
Their danger lies in using weapons forged
By evil men, or Satan, or his angels.
'Tis Satan's method to subdue the good
To use the weapons from heaven's arsenal.
This much, and valuable for sons of earth
To know, was learned by Satan in the war
With Michael and all Heaven's holy angels,
Whose issue might have doubtful been: but God

Appeared, and exercising infinite
Power, Satan and his crew discomfited
Became at once, were routed, put to flight,
And fell headlong like lightning into hell's
Abyss of liquid fire,—prepared long ere
The issue had been reached by Spirit Power.
Rebellion terminated now in Heaven
Eternally, and sweet peace reigned supreme.

   Earth speeds her journey to an issue like
To what in Heaven has been,—nor long delays,—
Compared to years eternal—nigh at hand!

   Their fall and rout from heaven's empyrean
Heights, lighted the universe like meteors,—
So numerous and swift was their descent.
A hand omnipotent controlled their flight
And guided them, none knowing whither led,
Or what their fate,—a secret, hidden hand,
Revealed alone to them in power and wrath!
For God in shape and form, or bodily,
Is seen by angels no more manifest

Than by man's finite powers,—in earth no less
Certainly than in Heaven's crystal plains.
Ere long they reached their place, nor long they fell
Though their descent was almost infinite,—
And lighted in our solar sphere, assigned
To them their prison of captivity!

BOOK III.

THE CREATION OF THE EARTH.

    WE bid farewell to sister planets, suns
And systems complicate through vast expanse
Of space, and come to learn how grew the earth
Into the perfect state which time reveals.
    From chaos void to morning light, and earth
Severed from other worlds, the firmament
Between, from gaseous state became a globe
Of fire, whose liquid waves hissed direfully
For thousands and ten thousand ages through
The abyss of space, borne on its giddy speed
As swift as since it's travelled, till cooled, brought
To solid state prepared for something new.
    Here was confusion,—burnings most intense
Befitting Satan and his angels lost

Since their sad banishment from heaven and bliss,
A literal hell-fire and brimstone, named
In Scripture upon which so many cavil, nay!
Wrest, alas! to their own dismay in future,
Counting it language simply figurative.
Let none delude themselves. There is a hell
Literal in fact as an earth and Heaven:
Also remorse of soul which hell may figure!
Bodies are circumscribed and must have place,
And finite spirit bodies through which to act,
Whether they're carnal or are spiritual.
Otherwise pantheists have views correct,
And spirits finite are but parts of God
To be again absorbed by Deity,
Like mists which to wide ocean depths return.
Thus personality is lost, destroyed,
And men like brutes will be annihilated,—
And none will venture proof that thus 'twill be
With e'en them, that they never reappear.
    Angels who lost their first estate, against
A bountiful Creator sinned, rebelled
Unprovoked, having no cause nor pretext.

'Twas crime atrocious, meriting no less
Judgment than banishment eternally
From God, and all the punishments endured!
Having for ages suffered for their sins,
And waking as from a dream, they beheld
The molten earth congealed to globe opaque,
And now engirdled by a shoreless sea
Whose boiling waves were driven from pole to pole
Like hissing serpents, horrid, venomous,
Innumerable, ploughing through the waste:
At times lifted high 'gainst the canopy
Of heaven, followed by the angry fire
Which warred beneath like hell's artillery.
This was the eve when all the frightful powers
Of dark commotion held the reins of death.
The ocean's tides then murmured not in notes
So soothing sweet as now unceasing heard,
Nor glowed in varied colors as the glad
Waves lift their crests on high, some glistening white,
Others in purple, some in azure tinge,
Or undulating green, the garb of spring;

For still the glorious rays of parent sun
Shone not through dense mists girdling all the earth.
   The angels coming from the depths of fire,
The abyss where long they'd lain in agony,
Beheld the change. Amazed each mutely stood
And eyed the other in blank astonishment.
'Twas Heaven compared to what they'd suffered long.
But consternation seized them, fearing some
New display of omnipotence, and worse
Fate possibly than yet endured. Hence each
And simultaneously dove into hell's
Abyss of liquid fire, to hide in earth's
Centre from God,—whose face and power they feared
More than the waves of liquid fire—their home,
With which long since they had become familiar!
Thus we've seen turtles in spring-time beneath
The water quickly dart and hide from fear.
   Still earth advanced—a brighter morning dawned—
A glimm'ring star that twinkled now amid
The suns and other worlds, a thing of life
That hung upon nothing in creation's morn,
Appeared the earth amid the other worlds,—

'Floating through ether sea most beauteously, —
Where splendors upon splendors beamed and shone
Translucent, glories upon glories streamed
From each, contributing a universe
Of wonder, beauty, blessings, and of praise
To Heaven's Great King, enthroned above the worlds!
    The proud waves were conquered by laws ordained
And gathered in one place, their bounds assigned.
The dry land quivering rose from the abyss
And held their universal tide at bay.
The vanquished waves of liquid fire roared loud
And hideously in death's agonies strong,
And one effort more made to break their chains.
Their gathering strength the earth and sea beheld,
Trembling. Ere long they came with thunder's roll
And grew intensely fierce with moanings dire.
The ocean heard, and fainting sunk away:
The feeble earth threw wide apart its gates,
And quick an o.'erwhelming flood possessed its walls.
Then rushing from beneath, their dread abode,
They labored hard to win the heaven's heights
To bring the reign of chaos back again;

From thence returned they rolled their molten waves
Upon the land, which gave an icy chill
That stayed their course. Hence wave upon wave was
    piled
Congealed to solid stone which mountains formed,
The granite chains to bind secure the earth's
Framework. Thus valleys, hills and mountains rose.

  Now Satan's voice resounded through the bowels
Of earth amid the roar of liquid fire.
Aroused was every spirit and intent
To hear, each welcoming a sound so long
Silent, familiar once and sweet to all.
Nor all its former sweetness yet was lost,
But harshly corresponding to the place
It roared compared to what in heaven erst
It was: Up, friends, assert again your rights.
Why longer here in abject bondage lie!
We thus abase ourselves below this hell
Infernal, where too long we've lain submiss
As though deserving worse, should heaven elect
To inflict. The earth and all the solar sphere,

The Creation of the Earth.

The planets, sun and every satellite
Are ours. No longer in this prison hell
And writhe in torture we'll remain, as though
Meek slaves content to bear all heaven wills !
We have the power which guarantees the right.
Let each and all repair to solid earth,
The surface habitable now and ours.
'Tis ours to reign in kingdoms here o'er earth
And every solar sphere, excepting none,
Now perfecting by laws in matter solely :
With which our enemy, who from the heights
Of heaven expelled us long ago, has naught
To do. We're masters here and this our heaven.

With Satan infidels agree, denying
That God controls development ; who claim
That laws explain, account for all that is ;
And wish to banish thought of God ; have license
To act their pleasure, irresponsible—
And die like brutes, become annihilate !
Yet Satan is more reverent than they
And more devout,—in that he ne'er denies

That God exists—though base he's not a fool.
If laws account for nature, what accounts
For laws—whence born—whose womb maternal gave
Them birth? Thus sceptics and false logic well
Agree, are plausible to compass bad
Design. But truth is better felt than known
By men who follow Satan's wake: abject
They make a show of wisdom which betrays
Them fools; and like to evil spirits are,—
Submiss to thus abuse their spirit power.

When called by Satan, towering above
All, high and eminent among the hosts,
None hesitated: all at once arose
Gladly, like convicts from their prison cells
And chains released, intent upon Satan's lead,
And roamed throughout the earth or visited
The neighboring moon or planets, or the sun.

Through all the ages subsequent the power
Of Satan dominant has been in earth.
Its wealth and honors he has claimed to give

To votaries who worship at his shrine.
Even our Lord, divine, who came from heaven
With power infinite to save earth and man
And elevate us to heaven's heights of glory,
Was impiously tempted, Scriptures teach,
By Satan, who the kingdoms of the earth,
Their grandeur, glory, power and wealth displayed
Before the Saviour's eye, a moment's time
Simply required, to whom the Tempter said,—
All these are thine, for mine they are to give,
And more, if thou wilt simply worship me!

   O! sad the fact, too manifest, that still
The earth belongs to Satan's votaries,
Who mainly hold its wealth and proudly reign
And riot, subject to their Mighty Chief!
Hence shade and darkness cover earth and sea
And pall the heart of man with gloom intense!
The beasts complain, and day is turned to night;
Groans follow shrieks where strifes successful reign;
Man's scent for blood scares creatures fierce, untamed;
The winds but wail; the waters voice but moans;
The mountains seem to cry and waterfalls

To rage; the clouds o'erspread the sky and mourn
Like houses for the dead,—all in despair!
Thus spirit power, in league with death, appals
The earth inanimate and man and beast!

    But light illumes the clouds if we'll but see—
And every cloud that casts a shadow o'er
Our life or earth or sea or universe!
The spirit power that casts a gloom excites
But moans, or crushes hearts and causes shrieks,—
Is under Power Supreme, which dominates!
For us there's need of sorrow and of shade;
For us earth moans, and clouds of heaven weep,—
Directing thought and heart to God and Heaven!
For us lambs bleed and creatures die, with looks
Of patience in their face, reproachfully!—
Directing thought and heart to Christ, the Lamb
Of Heaven, displaying attributes of love
And mercy new to angels—upon the Cross!
For us are these alarms, and men unkind
Give angry glare and looks of hate, and Satan
Too, tempting with hell's blandishments and
    arts,—

For then we fly into the arms of love,
Where safety is assured by Power Supreme!
    Thus in its light and shade is spirit power
Discerned for good and ill—but good prevails,
Subdues and uses ill for greater good!

BOOK IV.

THE CREATION OF PLANTS.

Now from the dreary past of fire and gloom
We come to sing of spring's engendering growth:
Not beauteous as now, but as each new stage
Developed more and more in higher life.
An omnipresent power superintends
The whole to accomplish the end first designed,—
An energy we cannot understand,
Hid deep within the veil of mystery.
  The Spirit absolute to us revealed
In works and ways which now we humbly sing,
Whom reverently we worship, is self
Dependent, penetrating everything,
Himself controlling all development
Unto a destiny which he has willed:

The Spirit independent, yet within
All things as souls inhabit flesh and form,
And still without, above and infinite.
He now his power exerts and life appears.
The peaks that look above the misty clouds,
The barren hills below and ocean's depths
Teem with organic life, now first produced.

'Tis here in vegetation, trees and flowers
That God in beauty best is seen, the only
Spirit Power that abides therein ; where each
Is perfect in itself; where Spirit less
Than God abides not, nor destroys, nor mars ;
Where God abides alone, the life and power
To build, construct, mature and beautify.
O, wonderful creation, body of
The Deity, how beautiful, how bright !
Oh ! then what is Eternal Loveliness,
The Spirit infinite which is the Life,
The Fount of all, revealed in all that is—
Himself alone without a fount, unborn !

Life's called a vital something undefined,
Subjecting nature's pre-existing laws :

Which lifts the drooping flower to taste the breeze,
And rears the cedar's giant form to brave
The tempest's force : a subtle, mighty power
Whose strange complexity none has resolved :
A centre round which nature's laws and all
The elements revolve to minister
While it develops.   Beautiful is life !
When gone, how changed the form in which it dwelt !
The giant oak with leaves and branches, trunk
And all as perfect as when life was there,—
But dead,—how changed and still ! The powers that erst
Were subject now assume their right to prey
And feed upon the ruins undisturbed.
Oh ! what a world of wonder in each flower
That lifts its shining head to see the sun.
O ! who can comprehend the vital power
That rests within the seed that germinates
Beneath the earth ! A wisdom infinite
Alone could guide the hidden mystery
In matter inorganic, and continue
Developing it, age rolling o'er age !

The Creation of Plants.

O, pilgrim, fellow of the toils of search
Through ages dark, and lone and patiently
We've travelled ages long o'er dreary seas,
If possible to reckon time ere life
Appeared, and seen the elements at war
To form the earth. As mariners we joy
To see the mountain tops and landscapes grow
Upon our gaze. But rest is distant far.
Still patiently and long we'll beat the waves
Of time to bring the distant shores in full
And perfect beauty clearly to our sight.

We now descend into the labyrinth
Of earth, deep in the darksome cells of death,
And leave the world above in glittering pomp,
Pleasure and pride, pursuing its own course;
While we below in solitude, a place
For thought, read the archives of nature past.
Recorded here is earth historic as
When first it wore its robes of emerald green.

We note first thallogens as seen beneath
The water ere the land had come to view,
With no ranunculi which glow in red,

Or lilies white which deck our placid pools ;
But stript of flowers and leaves they gloomily
Appear. Behold far, far above this stage
Of things and see the acrogens, with stems
And leaves, a growth luxuriant, varied, rich.
Some shallow banks with verdant mosses decked,
And plants most like those of Pacific isles
Where through the earth's diurnal course the spring
Glows warm, unvaried by cold northern blasts ;
And some low pools with ferns whose broad leaves once
Clothed green the Emerald isle, and now enrich
The hills and plains warmed by the tropic sun.
For then from northern chambers unexplored,
Eveloped then and still in mystery,
No winds cold like an avalanche of ice
Carried dire destruction in their train.
The earth, warmed by its own enveloping
Light above and internal fires beneath,
Felt a uniform glow through all its veins.
Then too the gorgeous forests waved in strength
Denser, mightier than the world since has seen.
Then grew in perfect strength the calamites,

The equiseta, lepidodendra tall
And beautiful, and arborescent trees
As stately as the Norfolk Island pines
And noble as the cedars, prince among
The trees, which grow upon Mount Lebanon.
Perfumes were not exhaled by flowers in spring,
The rose unborn was yet beneath the earth :
Nor had the polyanthos, nor the white
Violet so modest in its speaking worth,
Nor the anemone pale which loves the shade
Of groves, or any sweet flower yet appeared.
Nor were there birds to sing a lullaby
Rejoicing in the ever-shining day,
Nor beasts to roam the shady forests through.
How sombre, yet imposing was the scene !
Now rising in the scale the conifers,
Which darkened Scotland's moors and bare hillsides,
Lift their giant trunks proudly to the skies ;
And sigillaria spreading undisturbed
By other growth their mighty reign, their stems
With sculptures variously decked, fluted like
The Doric columns carved by Grecian hand.

These monuments of ancient grandeur all
Have passed away, their ruins only left.
As empires rise obscurely into strength
And flourish while the morning lasts, then sink
Gradual into decay, their ruins left
As legacies bequeathed to after-powers
To build a structure more advanced in might
And beauty, so the eve of day the third
Grew slowly into morn and brilliant shone
Until the light waned for the evening's shades.

    With such a gorgeous growth the ancient world
For myriad ages shone among the stars,
A mellow light. From north to south, from east
To west, where'er the land appeared above
The sea, the globe around, umbrageous trees
Gigantic sprang and grew vigorously
From tepid soil: the same that's buried now
Beneath our feet, compressed to crystal coal,
The mines of treasures inexhaustible
For the use of man. O, could ingratitude
Withhold our praise from the creative power
Who thus provided for our wants ere man

Created trod this paradise of earth?
Oh, let all who would magnify the Lord
Pursue with patient thought His mighty works!
Sceptic! why close your eyes to sink your soul,
So nobly formed for aspirations high,
Beneath the instinct of animal kind!

 In such a murky atmosphere, and light
Continuous enveloping the earth
By fires volcanic, in dense fogs and shade
The fallen angels walked or councils held,
And noted each progressive step from lower
To higher life, and talked of future plans
To make and hold the earth their Paradise.
Whene'er a new display of power Supreme
For further progress and advance in earth's
Construction, independent of all law,
Was felt or seen, then fearing and in awe
Of heaven's power invisible, which once
They'd felt, in abject terror each would flee
Seeking dense darkness, impenetrable,
In dens and caves, or through volcanic fires

And craters dive headlong into the bowels
Of earth to hide themselves! What next decreed
Ignorant of; hence always on the alert
To fly,—yet knowing not where to escape
From power and presence personal around
Them evermore to punish or refrain!
But Spirit Infinite withholding during
Long intervals His intervening power
Rendered the fiends bold, and reassured
They'd appear and presume their right to reign.

    Thus creature powers, malign, their shadows cast
Upon earth, which in both light and shade progressed.
Power infinite to bless is always light,—
But power finite, intent upon ill, is dark
And lowering, big with curse, surcharged with death!

BOOK V.

A SOLAR DAY AND YEAR BEGUN.

ANOTHER day now dawns upon the world.
The light that floated on the misty sea
Around the earth against the ethereal vault,
In silence gathered into waves and rolled
Within the tabernacle of the sun.
The murky vapor, screening every isle
And continent, so richly robed, from sight,
Felt northern blasts and gathered into clouds
And rain. The curtain drawn, the parent sun
Now first beheld to bless the blooming world.
How rapturous must every pulse have throbbed
When first it felt that gentle, bounteous hand!
The clouds arrayed themselves in azure tints;
The mountains seemed adorned with burnished gold;

The hills and plains looked up serenely sweet,
And smiled with more than lover's pride when first
The idol of his soul with fluttering heart
Bestows the long-delayed first kiss of love ;
The breeze in music's wild, subduing notes
Played wantonly among the glistening leaves ;
The streams enchanted sang their lullaby ;
The slumbering, lazy waves awaked to life
And rolled with noiseless flow to kiss the beach ;
The clouds, the mountains, and the hills and plains,
The oceans slumbering in the land's embrace,
And all the fulness of the earth rejoiced
To feel the thrilling light and heat of day.
Oh ! thou majestic sun, what beauty, power
And life thy every glorious beam displays :
How great, stupendous is thy potent reign !
The day declined ; the sun had travelled o'er
The ecliptic path ; then gathering his robes
Of state and beauty of vermilion tints,
Retired within the chambers of the west.

 The first night shone in light of silvery glow :
A light so calm that nature sinks within

A Solar Day and Year Begun.

Its folds and falls away in sweet repose,
Unconscious as a babe that sleeps upon
Its mother's breast. For while the mellow light
Of eve was lingering with its soothing touch,
Up rose the moon to rule as queen of night,
And rolled with steadfast splendor through the heavens.
Calm was her face unveiled, a beauty mild,
Serene, that melts night into seeming day;
As innocence and virgin purity
The heart intent upon a dark design.
Then followed on, the silent starry train
Attendant, waiting on her Majesty
Whose lustrous splendor scarce excels their own.
They decked the firmament of ether blue,
The robe of heaven, as gems of every shade.
Thus reigned successively the sun by day,
The moon and stars by night,—a solar day,
The first that dawned upon the earth, and still
Revolves the same to bless the race of man.
Then first began the seasons to assume
Their round of changes, each in beauteous robes
Distinct and varied through the rolling year.

Aries, the leader of the train, received
The now reviving sun of spring, when cold
And dreary winter, softened by the touch,
Withdrew reluctant from the land and sea.
Taurus, rejoicing in his seven stars
And Hyades which brightly radiate
His face, next followed in the starry host,
Accompanied by valiant Perseus, son
Of Jupiter, and Eridanus, king
Of rivers coursing serpentine through the heavens.
The embryo buds felt the mild influence,
And fearless of the biting frost unfolded
Their hidden treasure to perfume the breeze.
The tender grass began to spring and grow
In wild luxuriance, carpeting the earth.
All vegetation felt the new impulse
Propelling hidden life's development.
Following on the Ledean pair arose
Heralded by Auriga, charioteer,
And bright Orion, to receive the sun
And lead him through the closing months of spring.
The clouds charged heavily dropt down their showers

Of melting rain ; the rivers flooded full
Discharged their wealth into the spacious seas ;
The winds invigorating nature's growth
Blew calm and mild, a warm and pleasant breath.

    From Gemini the sun munificent
Rolls into Cancer, then as now betwixt
The Lynx and Hydra's sparkling eyes, whose folds
Are trailed along the sky full many a league.
And now while driving through this measured
    space
With equal speed, began to glow with more
Than its accustomed fire, and pour its rays
As liquid streams to deluge earth and sky.
The drifting clouds now intervene and pour
Their cooling rain upon the thirsting soil
That else would lose its verdure and become
A waste, a desert drear as Afric's sands.
Leo next followed in the bright array,
Courageous Judah's sign for victory.
While in this province tarrying the sun
Glows hot, and nature coils beneath its power,
The blaze intenser than through the long year.

Then Astrea gracefully escorts the king
Through her domains and ends the silver months.
    Summer closed, yellow autumn 'gins to smile,
Combining all the varied beauty, strength
And luxury advancing through the signs ;
Evenly weighed when the Golden Scales are seen
To hold the sun, whose journey 'mong the stars
Then half accomplished sheds the light of day
Of equal length with night upon the earth.
Next baleful Scorpis, rising with the sun,
And Sagittarius refulgent ends
The season for the coming winter months.
    When Capricorn is reached and seen among
The stars, clouds darken earth and storms begin
And vegetation's beauty fades and dies.
Aquarius rising next consigns the earth
To barren winter's cold and rigid reign.
Then Pisces closing up the starry train
Brings milder rays upon the frozen earth,
And soon it feels reviving spring again.
    Thus in successive order placed, the stars
Became the signs for seasons equally

Balanced, and closed the fourth and lovely day,
When in the firmament the sun became
Earth's light by day, the moon and stars by night,
Combined each year the same harmoniously.

   By bright dissevered worlds and suns which shine
Nightly we're lured from earth to crystal plains
And purple fields and amber hills and mounts
Of gold, as if our home's beyond, above!
We yearn to soar outside of space, to climb
The highest peaks on which a Paradise
We dream and feel and hope may be enjoyed.
Earth does not feed enough, nor satisfy,
More than a nest a bird with wings full fledged.
   In God is home, and He's somewhere concealed,
We feel, in sweeter vision than the earth
Affords, within the starry realms which nightly
Twinkle in myriad lights of diamond lustre,
But noiselessly—in silence from the sky.
But God is near, as well in earth as stars
Beyond, and we're inclined for Him to look
Above, and dream and pray to come where He

Abides,—when He's in Person at our side!
But many see Him not, and know not where
To look :—in mountain caves where pilgrims pray;
In hovels of the poor where poverty's
Unfelt in daily praise for bounties given;
In chambers where meek sufferers lie with Heaven's
Halo upon their brow, in patient waiting
The appointed hour of dissolution's touch—
For golden chariots, whose wheels they hear
Afar, and angel messengers to bear
Them hence,—oh! there in Person God abides,
And there is seen, and felt, and touched, and loved,—
Which every craving of the soul doth meet!

  Through our tears we often see Him drawing near!
He rather seeks for us, a home within
Our hearts—is more inclined thereto than we
To seek a home, a heavenly rest, in Him!
We are in Him and He in us if helped
And comforted upon our way to Zion!
Oh! then our vision will be unobscured
In starry ether blue, where worlds do shine
Without a cloud, without the blight of sin!

A Solar Day and Year Begun.

Ah! hence our souls, when yearning for the stars,
Are true to nature, and but speak the speech
Of spirit dialect for purity!

    The evil spirits had resumed their office,
And busily had every spot explored
Upon earth's surface, every continent
And isle and sea, and every grove and forest.
The beauty of the day and night, illumed
With rays of heavenly light, admiringly
They revelled in, forgetful of their lost
Estate and liability to worse
Punishment than yet they'd endured in hell
If aggravated crimes should be enacted.
Their nature now was sinfully inclined,
As man's unless restrained by power divine.
The dazzling splendor of the heaven's light,
Or earth's beneficence, or their release
From lakes of fire, excited no pure thought
Or sense of gratitude. Their hearts, inured
To woe, had hardened more and more, and cold
Had grown as icebergs, heaven's sweet rays withheld.

The fact of earth's developing as seen
By them from molten waves to solid earth;
From liquid fires into cool lakes and seas,
And mountains, hills and plains,—more beauteous
As time rolled on—a happy dwelling-place,
Had more than fires infernal rendered hard
And stubborn and defiant their wills fallen.
As centuries rolled over centuries
And time interminable seemed, their state
And place becoming better and not worse,
Their nature more defiant grew against
Authority, as when dethroned from Heaven.
So man, the more abject his poverty,
If raised to independence, wealth or fame,
Is arrogant, intolerant, self-poised,
Except restrained by God mercifully.

  Satan, who gloried now in being called
Beelzebub, deemed this a fitting time
To hold a council and inaugurate
A new rebellion, and devise what plans
Were best to overcome whate'er is good
Or pure or holy in the earth or heaven.

Great was the convocation now convened,
Which seemed a forest newly sprung to life
Upon a continent interminable.
And still from regions far in companies
They came, like clouds obscuring heaven's light.
Their voices multitudinous were like
The ocean, storm-tossed, rolling on the beach.
Satan at last arose and carefully
The heights empyrean intently scanned,
And seeing no more on the wing, enjoined
Silence. The roll called,—none failed to respond.
Satan, well pleased, in grandeur rose and stood
Before the multitude as formerly
In heaven, a mighty prince adored by all.
A shout spontaneous was given which crashed
Upon the heavens as though colliding worlds
Had brought the reign of chaos back again !
Each visage dark was now intent to hear
The counsel and command of their great chief.

 As once Elijah upon Mount Carmel stood
Before all Israel, king and councillors,
So Satan now, the mighty chief of fallen

Angels, and thus addressed the multitude :—
Friends, each a prince in this realm, patiently
Hear mysteries which Spirit Power reveals,
And hearing act for safety and defence,
For sovereignty, renown and victory.
Nature with capabilities for good
Or evil is endowed :—two powers contend
For mastery,—the evil with the good,
The impure with the pure, and hell with heaven.
Hence light and darkness, calm and tempest, fire
And smoke, and Heaven and Hell. As spirits fallen
We are esteemed by Michael and his hosts,
The antipodes. Against his kingdom war
Eternally we must declare and wage.
Creation's work is going on, and earth
Developing, as each may easily
Perceive, and doubtless will continue long,—
Earth will become a paradise of sweets,
Growing more perfect finally reach Heaven.
Then we'll be driven to another hell,
Doubtless worse than the one we've here escaped.
Our work hence is clear, to promote the evil

And overthrow the good, and make the earth
Instead of Heaven a hell. Whatever comes
From the Creator's hand is always good.
We're fools and blind if we cannot perceive—
Our work must be to render morally
And physically hurtful everything ;—
To make our kingdom stronger than the angels',
More potent than the heavenly ;—to spread
Barrenness, droughts and storms ;—to multiply
Whate'er is noxious in both plants and beasts—
And germs already are developing,
If I divine aright, the germs just formed,
Such as the universe has never seen,—
An animal creation above the plants.
Exert your spirit power,—become as Gods
And each a God and reign, subduing good !
These germs possess ;—their bodies shape and form
Into the most repulsive creatures e'er
Conceived ;—their spirit power excite to hate,
And render greedy to devour, corrupt,
Malignant, and inaugurate in earth
Among the animal tribes bloody wars.

We'll feast our souls continual thus in strifes,
And Heaven's spirits will desert the place.
All finite spirit, rule and render foul,—
Possess, corrupt and render powerful
Their bodies to destroy their enemies,
And even malintent against their kind !
Excite in all a spirit to destroy !
With putrefying carcasses fill earth
And sea ! Thus every form of good subdue,
And enter eagerly upon the task,—
A happy one to vanquish every foe !
Our interest demands, our pleasure prompts
To keep the earth from reaching perfect bliss
And make it more and more the antipode !

  Ne'er was war declaration given which so
Amazed and silenced every beating heart.
'Twas admiration and consent so free
And full that happiness in every bosom
Reigned—a kind natural to fallen angels—
So new since long their banishment from Heaven
And in accord with their impulse for evil,
That every one stood as though fettered strong

In gloom, where darkness reigns and holds supreme
Control throughout their universal realm !
Their sentiments at last expressed themselves.
Shout followed shout continuous, so long
And loud it seemed a carnival of blood.
All hell's discordant moan and wail were sweet,
Confusion order and gloom light compared !

   Most modern preaching and beliefs, too much
We fear, the devil's agency in earth
And man ignore, forgetful of what Christ
Our Saviour taught and did with them while here !—
Forgetfulness that pleases Satan well,
And mightily his kingdom helps 'mong men !
Many apologists has Satan here !
Some, e'en the watchmen who on Zion's walls
Claim faithfully that they fulfil their office,
To blow the trump and warn against surprise,
Fail to discern Satan's foul agency
In gross and heinous crimes by men committed,
Deeming that human nature fallen, to sin
Inclined, for all sufficiently accounts.

Thus men are fooled and devils helped to reign !
O, watchmen ! dangers are abroad and death !
Be vigilant and faithful, true and bold !
Soft words and speeches may deceive, betray,—
And cost a soul its death—yourselves the guilt !

    Dark earth has rays divine from Heaven's throne.
Her vale of tears responds to soothing touch
When pastors, heaven-commissioned saints, stand forth
Betwixt the living and the dead, to speak
For God and purity and bliss divine.
Solemn and sacred is the trust, and rich
Will be their crown if faithful to the end.
They stand where cherub angels fain would serve
To plead in sympathy with common guilt
And show the way from sorrow, sin and death,
To joy and holiness and bliss and Heaven.
Their virtues hath a tongue which checks earth's pride,
Their dignity a power subduing men,
Their independence of the world a voice
Proclaiming them the legates of high Heaven.
To God and not to men subordinate,
And ne'er obsequious for worldly ends ;

Willing to bear reproach, privation, pain
Or death to help and bless and save mankind;
The messengers of mercy to the lost;
Solicitous to plead with angel power,
And feel and weep like babes where sorrow reigns,
They're guardian angels clothed with power sublime
To execute, ne'er legislate, the laws
Which Heaven legislates for guilty earth,—
Intent alone that their commission holy
And their credentials clear shall be from God.
In right inflexible. When cares invade
Or wrongs assail, with strength divine they're spurned.
To be enthralled too lofty is the soul,
And absolute God's word to be annulled.
Hence pastors plead that life and liberty,
That glorious release from human chains
May be awarded rightly to the slave
Which guilty man has bound and caused to bleed!
Profoundly penetrated by the truth,
Born in the bosom of the Infinite,
A pastor stands before the world a guide
With trembling finger pointing to the skies,

Aglow with zeal, intensely moved to save,—
A zeal proportioned by the years to come
And possibilities of spirit here
And evermore in realms beyond the grave!
In love with Christ, constrained and purified
Thereby, like Him they love the sons of men.
The darkest spot where sin and sorrow cry,
Where human nature bleeds in agony,
A faithful pastor's presence renders bright,—
Upon whom e'en dying eyes will turn and smile,
Responsive to a loving hand, and words
Of sympathy which drop from tender lips! .
A pastor's heart throbs lovingly for men
In all the ills of life, and yearns to help,
As Jesus wept and dried the tears of grief
In other eyes at mourning Bethany!

  Sorrowing souls, struggling for release from bonds
And tendencies, desires impelling them
To sin, to which their natures bend as trees
Before a gale, or from the Tempter's power,
O! Spirit, Paraclete, our Living God,
Help such to overcome their deadly foes,

That earth may be a thing of beauty, place
Surpassing sweet, while they sojourn below!
O, Fountain! source of unction—holy love,
Give strength for weakness, fortitude for fear,
And wisdom for their creature ignorance!
May they in spirit soar where angels dwell
And revel in Elysian fields of light,
By help of Thee vouchsafed, above these ills,
Beyond the Tempter's wiles, where Thou dost reign
Alone, in regions far removed from night—
Where distant far are seen the realms of shade,
Like clouds that hang upon the brow of space!
Thus rule, Almighty One! reveal Thy power
In light, as fallen spirits do in shade!
Surely our struggling race is helped of Thee
When light from darkness dawns within the soul!

BOOK VI.

CREATION OF ANIMALS.

IN lands of mystery thus far we've travelled,
And realms of wonder new and strange disclosed
From dark chaotic void to light and heat
Which flood the earth with blessings marvellous,
And near our native shores with gladdened heart.
We'll travel, pilgrim, still o'er stony paths;
Through desert sands, both barren, hot and drear;
And mountain glens, where dangers seem to warn
At every step, where much will pain the heart
And sicken sight, from which we'll turn away
In horror or disgust, and seek a place
To hide or rest our weary, troubled souls:
But here and there we'll meet, as in the past,—
Upon a turn and unexpectedly,—

A bright oasis ; or a grateful shade ;
Or some clear sparkling fount, with music sweet ;
Or limpid streams, refreshing weary limbs
And cooling heated brows, and cleansing too ;
Or meads where sportive flocks in safety graze !
From darkness, light will break ; from ills when all
Seems lost, will good appear ; so shade and light,
And good and ill will alternate in time
To come as in the past,—for thus is life,—
For thus is earth,—for thus is pilgrimage
Below—to dawn in one eternal day,
Where all is bright and fair, a fountain full
Of light, reflecting shades of myriad hues—
To end in Heaven, without a cloud, where pains
And trials, weariness and deaths are o'er !

As mists before the rising sun withdraw
We see the wonders of mysterious power
Enlarged—enjoyment added now to life.
Sensation marks the new created world.
From regions where the glistening Polar ice
As mountains rise into the central zone,

To where the equator's ring volcanic runs
The round of earth, the oceans from their deep
And silent tomb up to their restless waves,
The land from level undulating plains
To where are regions of eternal snow,
An animal life joyous moves through the whole.
The forests dense possessed by creatures huge,
Voracious beasts; the waters luminous
With their unnumbered hosts; the burdened air
Scarce holds the clouds of life; the myriad flocks
Of fowl of every shape and size eclipse
The light of heaven and darken land and sea,
Depending upon the Spirit Power, whose hand
Bountiful gives the blessings which each needs.

 We here behold benevolence displayed
Through every channel of created life,
A goodness seen to grow through every stage,—
Advancing like the unassuming rill
Into vast streams, impetuous, uncontrolled:
Goodness embracing power omnific, first
Displayed, omniscient wisdom next revealed!
The o'erwhelming tide of bliss which swells within

The mighty worlds and quivers through the veins
Of breathing life, creative good reveal
And Spirit Power, which all the wise discern.
   Grovelling and sluggish are the pigmy souls
Which in a drowsy, dreamy state delude
Their better sense and turn their eyes away
From light, refuse to see the agency
Divine pervading nature's laws, the mode
In which the Spirit Power constructs the earth
For man to inhabit! Man, impertinent,
Excuses Heaven's Majesty, whose mind
Pervades immensity, from all concern
Of things below,—eliminates the God
Of nature from all nature's laws, ordained
Of Him! Absurd,—for infinite, no more
Is He in Heaven above than in the earth
Beneath. The infant at the mother's breast
Shames while we pity these perverted souls!
Revolting and sad is the state of those
Who glory in their shame; who light a torch
That men may clearly see their nakedness!
Such independent glory in themselves

And thus too sink below the grade of fools.
If God did not control the forming world
And energize the whole, how first appeared
The breathing animal in perfect type,
Each species beautifully formed, developed,
When first it saw the light or breathed the air?
Reason, aside from Scripture, ne'er concedes
To subtle laws of plants inhering power
To generate the beasts which roam the fields
Or fish inhabiting the sea's domain.
Yet fancies are conceived no less grotesque
Than they're absurd, irreverent, which teach
Us so,—and further trench upon a weak
Credulity by laboring hard to prove—
Their theory and selves consistent here—
That monkeys are progenitors of men
By law aside from Spirit.Power Supreme.
The law, intelligent, they never name.
If sceptics, in form men, have origin
With such a vulgar type of animals,
Ever most deftly do they conceal their tails;
Yet such appendage needs become their kind:—

Nor thus were they by their ancestors taught—
Scarcely consistent with the theory,
To ignore their parentage by such concealment!
O! shame to mortal men responsible
Who thus degrade their powers and fail to see
Design and unity in every thing.
Away with fancies so absurd and base
Which thus construe the laws of God, enforced
That we may exercise intelligence.
Can insignificant devils entomb
The Mighty God, Creator of the heavens
And earth? or banish Him from earth's domain,—
Whose terrible word called it into space
And sent it forth to plough the azure deep?
If He, the Ever-Present, superintends
The work, this great theatre's wondrous life
Rises with steady tread, magnificent,
Into a perfect whole,—all harmony.

    For breathing life distinguished is this fifth,
A new day, thus distinct from all the rest.
We recognize the generative word
Which spoke life into being multiform,

And rendered each a perfect organism,
Each one a world of wisdom by itself,
Each kind distinct from germs originated
Solely by Spirit Power, the God of heaven.

   And now to read the world's past history
Again we tread the universe of death,
Descend again into the sepulchre
And there investigate a life extinct.
In strata buried for long ages past
Are written living truths which God, Supreme
Architect, there records ; each page and word
Reveals transcendent thought and mighty power.
'Tis ours most patiently to interpret all,
And thus ourselves advance in spirit power,
One end designed in the stupendous works.
Not done in a moment as we, prescribed
To time, are with childlike simplicity
Accustomed to look upon the display
Of power, but in ten thousand ages past :—
For what is time to the eternal King !
How short the intervening ages since

The solar wheel began to turn till now,
If multiplied successively by all
The years consumed by the age of every star,
To God's eternal years in darkness hid,
Pavilioned in the shades of mystery!
How small the space from earth to sun compared
With that betwixt the luminary globe
Without the milky-way upon the outskirts
Of space: and what this to infinity!
Shall finite mind prescribe the Infinite?
Can mortal thought dictate the time that God
Should do His work? Did He, the Architect
Of this earth habitable, when employed
In forming it, regard man's finite powers
To judge how His Might should best be displayed?
As children let us view our Maker's works,
And stand in dread awe of the mystery
That's hid behind the veil impenetrable!
Our souls which only here begin to glow
May thus grow brighter with ascriptions high.
Enough we have to learn within our scope
Of vision, ordered thus of God to employ

Our minds immortal, destined to expand
Throughout eternity, though now confined
To earth and body so symmetrical.
E'en in the cradle of our birth we plume
Our wings to soar throughout the vast profound
Of the universe to learn the wisdom, far
Beyond our mortal ken, displayed in orbs
Which nightly light the firmament of heaven,
And shed influence far, both sweet and mild.
E'en already ere our sojournment ends,
Impatient we discourse their magnitude,
The beaten paths they tread, their distance great
Or small compared, and weight,—which more inflames
Our souls than savory meats the hungry palate.
But here we ne'er can learn with certainty
Whether each is palatial rich, adorned
With clouds luxurious, mountains, hills and plains
As earth ; or souls immortal there inhabit,
With bodies clad, adapted to their spheres.
The future life these truths will render clear !
    Earth is a laboratory to employ
The powers of each succeeding race of men,

And each discover something new; a mine
Of wealth which never fails to yield its ores,
So precious to the soul, to those who dig
Untiring, undistracted by the sight
Of tinsel toys, and ply their noble work,
Both night and day, through sunshine and in storm;
A book whose leaves support the present world
Of beauty: the unfolding leaf by leaf
Of which to read shall still engage our thought.

 The mother earth in her bliss conjugal
But briefly slumbered with the parent sun ·
Inactive. God's command again compelled
Her fruitful womb to yield the wondrous life
Implanted by His power in hidden germs,
Which Satan had discovered long ago,
Both male and female, to which the command
Was given to be fruitful, multiply
And fill the land and seas, each of their kind.
Few traces of the life which then arose
In living species at this day exist:
Ere man was born their sun in darkness set.

But now enshrined in stone their petrified
Remains exist entire,—they mute mementoes
Of empires whose beauty, pride and strength, once—
Ah, once! how solemn is this tolling word—
Flourished; every empire of life a world
As seen emerging from the old that's past.

    The eaglet's drooping wings the parent bird
Perceives, and darts beneath her young to bear
Them on her own, lest overcome they faint
And fall: thus the accompanying Spirit's voice,
Which nightly holds me intercourse, inspires
My heart with courage to portray this world
Of life, the fifth from the Creator's hand.
O, pilgrim! follow, nor sustain a fear
To travel where God's hand hath wrought with power,
And where His steps have been in majesty!

    And God said, Let the waters in the seas
And on the land produce abundantly
The creatures having life to move and breathe
Within their element. And fowl were made
To fly in the air and open firmament

Of heaven. By monstrous whales the seas were swollen.
Dragons became unsightly in the deep.
And every living creature small and great,
And every wingéd fowl after his kind
Into active life and full being came.

    And God saw everything He made was good,—
Whate'er from infinite beneficence
Comes, when not misapplied by creature power,
Is always good or beautiful or holy,—
And blessing said, Be fruitful, multiply:
For God, divine, to say or will is one.
Scripture addresses man in human speech. .
The germs created are but once, develop
And propagate thereafter by the laws
Ordained: nor re-created if destroyed.
Straightway the seas were swollen with animals
And animalculæ, each one distinct,
And in inconceivable multitudes
So dense the waters turned as into blood,
As anciently the Nile when cursed of God:
And each though so minute enjoys its life.
The coral animals begin to build

Their paradise of beauty deep beneath
The roaring, rolling waves; the barren shoals
Of sand and solid rock were thus transformed
As into a garden of verdure, rich
In palaces, whose walls and corridors
Seem curtained with the richest drapery;
Whose floors of white sand are bespangled o'er
With shells; and through whose branching columns
    play
Little fish radiant in their crimson scales—
A habitation where the Nereids dwell.
These marvellous structures when complete appear
Above the waves as floating fairy isles,
Whose beach is strewn with sands of snowy white,
The surface clothed in green perpetual
Of tropic growth luxuriant; while within
The centre basks clear lakes or seas: above
No less enchanting than the crystal deep.
The Polynesian Archipelago
Thus is formed, islands which Pacific's waves
Ne'er can rend from their base, constructed e'en
By the least creatures which the human eye

Discerns.   The seas primeval not alone
Remarkable for such feeble architects,
For fish innumerable, both small and great,
In shoals move through the yielding element.
They congregate according to their kind
And spurn to associate with other tribes.
As clouds of different hues at setting sun,
So seem their shining scales upon the sea,—
Some shoals of burnished gold, some silvery tinged,
Or green or purple colored every shade.
Together they repel the foe or make
Attack, mailed thick with massive armor strong,
And weapons for defence, or else to o'erpower
And torture their conquered prey : far unlike
The species, harmless when compared, that now
Exist.   But some with bright enamelled scales
And graceful fins, of gentle habits, play
Together happily among the groves
Luxuriant on the ocean's floor, and feed
Upon the sweet tender herbs undisturbed.
The waters being warm and sluggish, most
Needed scales thick to endure their element.

Some single, of prodigious bulk and length,
When lying still as towering rocks beat back
The sullen waves ; or moving speedily
The waters boil discordant in their wake ;
Or when hungering, they give chase and raise
A tempest, their red jaws distended wide
To enclose their prey with a thunder crash !
Carnage when once begun is not allayed
Till every gory wave has been engorged.
Thus ocean's wide domain has been a dread
Theatre of bloodshed from first possessed
By animal life : not as fabled myths
Conceived, that prior to the fall of man
Unknown was strife and death to earth's creatures,—
For their fangs to kill also tortured too !
To man when pure exemption from the pangs
Of death was promised, while obedient.
Without man's quick assent the devil ne'er
Would have had power to reign in human souls !

   Every creature having simply life
And instinct, to preserve, perpetuate

And enjoy being, was an easy prey
Or tool to govern in evil angel hands.
Devoid of conscience, even when mature
Subject to Satan's will and powerless.
Of conscience unpossessed as yet was life,
And hence the way for Satan's victory
O'er them was sure unless restrained by God.
So Christ, the world's great Teacher, taught our race
While in the country of the Gergesenes,
By giving heed to earnest prayer by devils
Made, suffering them to possess a herd
Of swine when cast from lunatics by power
In Him inhering, Son of God, divine.
The swine, controlled by devils now, their own
Destruction sought, and madly rushed with one
Accord into the sea and perished in
The wat'ry deep. 'Twas also possible
Alike and credible, if during earth's
Formation, spirits, powers and potentates,
Intent upon making here a struggle fierce
For victory over whate'er is good,
Possessed the different kinds and types, new germs

Of creature life, when found developing,
To mould and fashion into noxious beasts.
From elements, since angels power possess
To form and move in bodies like to men,
As two, ere Sodom was destroyed, sojourned
With Lot and in the city doomed to fire,
'Tis not incredible should evil spirits
Form noxious beasts to desolate the earth.
'Twas wisdom hell conceived, to overcome,
Subvert and vanquish all the powers of heaven,—
Befitting Satan—worthy of his powers!

    Many of gentle, timid nature, lovely
In form and spirit, 'scaped the watchful eye,
Though ever on the alert, of evil angels,
And now are cherished by the race of man.
Satan nor angel is ubiquitous:
Either directly or through other spirits
They operate to compass their designs.
If individuals are rendered fierce,
When otherwise the nature of their kind,
Separately they are possessed and governed
By spirit independent of themselves.

'Gainst these the venom and malignity
Of devils from the dark abyss of hell
Is gratified and fed by having beasts
Voracious prey upon and gorge their blood—
The latter creatures of Satanic power
From the infancy of their kind in earth—
To Satan like in spirit and employ.
Also against the purest sons of men
They ever hurl their keenest darts, and ne'er
Relent when agonies endured by them
Both pall and sicken even earth with gloom!

    Though death reigns over innocent and fierce
Alike, yet Satan solely renders it
Calamitous. 'Tis bliss to live or die,
In either case depending upon the use
Of normal powers in healthy exercise:
Doubtless their dying happier than their birth
If uncorrupted by Satanic powers,—
Truth illustrated by chrysalides
Developing into bright butterflies.
Within our casket, when unsightly, old,

Decrepit it becomes, the body worn
And feeble, there exists a spirit form—
A body like the angels beautiful—
The old, like husk enclosing precious fruit,—
Vast possibilities to be developed,
When from the flesh and clay by death released,
Which to a wondering world will be revealed :
A stage advanced above our present life.
But Spirit Power is requisite.   No force
In matter lurks to render butterflies
Other than worms if reproduced by law
Inherent.   So man shuffling off this form
Assumes a higher life, which if sustained
In future life, becoming cherub-like,
In beauty gorgeous will give God the glory !
Hence shocking is the theory, that man,
Because related to the animal
World, is developed from and for the earth
Alone and by laws purely natural,—
Subverting Scripture, reason, sentiment
Common and universal 'mong our kind.
Such science, falsely so called, vitiates

Itself and violates the laws of thought.
The more a creature lives in sense alone
The farther he withdraws himself from God,
Who's Spirit pure enthroned above the known,—
Yea! from self-spirit power, our only source
Of bliss inhering in our nature fallen.
Hence creatures born by power divine to die
Ultimately, in no degree or sense
Proves God the author of calamity.
Himself pure spirit, holy, infinite
Alone in every attribute of Being,
Is lovely far above what heart conceives,—
And nothing does but what is good and pure,—
Which heaven to reveal holds in reserve.
Here sin and Satan render death a sting!
But thanks to God who giveth even us,
Who've sinned, a victory through Christ our Lord!
Much more if pure and holy, born to die,
Would death have been our blissful hour on earth,—
Unfolding life in higher, happier stage,—
Developing from bud into the flower,—
From mortal body into spirit form,

Immortal, like to Christ our Lord, in Heaven,—
Whose beauty on the Throne in Spirit body,
From flesh and clay assumed when death released
Him from the world, the eye of sense obscured
And rendered John as dead beneath its rays!

    Whatever creature, plant or beast or man,
In kind or types distinct, imperfect taints
Possess—are noxious, evil, hateful—this
Is not the work of God, in spirit pure,
But of the devils from the dark abyss,
And bear the mark of Satan and his angels.*
Our Saviour in His teachings once alone
To unbelieving hearts imparts this truth,
When healing by His touch a woman bound
Of Satan, lo, for eighteen years. Strange words
Were these from loving lips to Jewish ears.
And strange they may appear in modern times
To many little disciplined in thought—
Assured of everything save ignorance.

---

  * Victor Hugo describes the Devil Fish as "a huge glutinous mass, with a demoniac will."

Creation of Animals.

The hypocrite addressed by Him assumed
To teach the Master and the synagogue,
Was ruler in the church and first opposed
The work of Spirit Power in vanquishing
The devil and his agency on earth.
So too the devils-rendered lunatic
Often, exceeding fierce and dangerous,
Those they possessed among men: how much more
Their power and certain over beasts or birds
Or whate'er else they please to mould and rule!
The devils are in animosities,
In wraths, iniquities, in tempests, storms
And clouds which threaten earth or heaven,—not God
In exercise of power, who's lovely, good
And glorious, the light of spirit worlds
Which sport and move throughout the universe
In blissful freedom, God therein best known
By e'en the angels gathered at His throne.

The unstable continents and islands, washed
By warm and tropic waves from pole to pole,
And fanned by sickening torrid winds, are varied

With valleys, irrigated by warm streams
And murky lakes, enclosed by hills or plains
With forests of the cypress, yew or fir:
An even temperature from north to south.
A hideous reptile race with labor writhe
And crawl, as if just oozing into life
From out the filthy mire. Appalling is
Their magnitude. When each successive coil
Evolves, and stretched they lie full many a rood
Along the marshes, if seen human sense
Would faint and sicken at the horrid sight.
'Twere black and ugly fiends, fond of filth,
The lowest, most malignant which possessed
And formed and ruled the horrid reptile race—
Fact attested clearly by Mother Eve.
Such massive lizards either walk the land
Or swim the deep ; while some bask leisurely
Upon the sandy shores, deposit eggs
Abundant to fill earth with their huge tribes.
Enormous crocodiles also here show
Their frightful bulk upon the gloomy bays.
Their eyes, impatient for an enemy

And battle fierce and carnage, strife and blood,
Glare in the open space with angry fire,
Like fiends,—when engaged in deadly strife
Most happy, only intent to destroy :
As armies hostile, pressed on by the rear,
In strife continue till they lifeless lie
Upon the plain : or as electric clouds
With heaven's artillery charge, till all their force
Is spent, then vanish : thus, an enemy
Engaged, in mingled gore together bound
They writhe and twine about in horrid coils
For agony, as limb from limb is torn,
Their panoply of horny scales is broken,
Their armor torn away, but ne'er give o'er
Till each the other's entrails find and tear,
And each carcass lies strewn upon the plains.
The iguanodon in tangled jungles
Is seen, the largest reptile yet produced,
Upon the land king as leviathan
Is of the deep. Among the bogs and rank
Weeds megalosauri lurk to secretly
Spring and secure gigantic tortoises

Creation of Animals.

Or frogs, whatever unaware approach
Within their reach : and scorpions hid beneath
The fallen trees or rocks, from whence their black
Claws quick extend to seize their frightened prey.
Such horrid lizards fierce inhabited
The groves and swamps and lakes of continents,
Now high above the then encroaching sea.
Some such of size diminished still exist
In Galapagos Archipelago,
Under the equator, a pre-Adamite
World. But to some of this reptilian race
Were added wings to soar the air and pierce
The clouds sublime ; to perch upon the high
And snowy peaks, and glare their brazen eyes
Into the azure sky. These dragon forms
Colossal, stranger than in ancient myths,
And more grotesque than poets ever dreamed,
Seem fiends from the Stygian lake escaped
And come to view the earth and see how near
It reaches Paradise and blissful realms
From whence they'd been expelled,—intent to rule
The world. But these huge monarchs of the air,

So marvellous, began to vanish when
Another tribe assumed their element.
    The fiends luxuriated to possess
And fashion, mould and govern a higher kind,
Like hideous harpies, bodies like to birds
With feet and claws, but faces nearly human,
Such as the ancients in their myths conceived.
Gigantic fowl in myriads filled the air
Like clouds, or swam in flocks upon the shoals,
Or moved with oary feet upon the clear
Bosom of lakes and seas, or filled dense groves
Of pine and arborescent and tall fern .
When night began to draw her darkening cloud
Around the perfecting earth, whose guttural clang,
As lulling each his mate into repose,
A harsh clang from unnumbered throats combined
Inharmonious, rendered eve's stillness wild.
The busy bee, but few as yet, now first
Began to murmur in prophetic tones,—
The future world of flowers is drawing nigh.
The beautiful palm, the harbinger of peace,
Arose meekly from out the humid soil,

The crownéd king of the vegetable world.
Thus ended bright the morn of day the fifth,
Against devices devils used to hinder
God's work, to perfectness advancing still;
Whose evening and noon were characterized
By monsters unsightly, their natures fierce;
And vegetation suited to an air
And soil both warm and damp,—where frogs prevailed,—
A paradise reptilian—not for man
Adapted—still a charnel-house of death.

   The finishing touch from the Architect
Omnipotent now earth receives, and teaches
That power originates in spirit solely.
The natural from the spiritual subsists,
Without excepting aught that's seen or felt.
No substance has power other than bestowed,
Incorporate, by spirit pre-existent.
Hence force in matter latent may exist
For centuries and evermore, unless
By spirit liberated in the use

Of means : thus coal if kindled liberates
Force, as also water turned into steam ;—
But spirit acts to liberate the force :
The self-same pre-existent force evolves,
Is liberated, which at first was used
To give it form, but acts otherwise simply
Than that which formed the coal or element :
Simply reversed, like wire springs uncoiled
Evolve like force, the same which gave them tension.
Matter is inert. Spirit solely gives
Or liberates the force or power bestowed
Originally by Omnipotence.

    The different stages of creative work
Are drawing to a close. How rich the field
For thought we've travelled o'er—how full of praise !
We enter now as in a cool retreat,
A safe lagoon of fairy coral isles,
And view with joy the prospect beautiful.
    And God said, Let the earth bring forth, each after
His kind, the cattle, creeping things and beasts
Of the earth after their kind : and it was so.

Creation of Animals.

A new and higher world of life appeared.
Creatures innumerable by Spirit Power,
Created was each germ, and now developed
Lay half unconscious, and awoke to life
As from a dream, and looked upon the ground
And trees, and quaffed the fragrant air with strange
Delight. Instinctively they then began
To move their limbs; discovered power to rise.
Each sought his mate to multiply their kind,
For such their nature was: and some in pairs
Or herds, while others singly scoured the plains:
While flocks of birds and insects spread abroad
Their wings and sailed upon the ambient air.

Now all the beasts and everything that creepeth
The earth, were made,—their nature formed to enjoy
A mode of life distinct in every kind.
Most still exist, but some have passed away.
Behemoth sluggishly then lay concealed
In reeds and fens, or walked the mountain sides;
The dinotherium and the mastodon
Colossal, and the mammoth shaggy-haired,
Through forests dense and wide devoured the shrubs

And trees, together with the elephant,
Most gentle, noble in his mighty strength
When unmolested, terrible when roused
By foes, which scarce 'scape his sagacious tact;
The untractable rhinoceros, against
Whose thick skin, as coat-of-mail, weapons sharp
Rebound, wallowed unwieldy in the marsh;
Or river-horse, amphibious, among
Stately grown reeds walked, or with sullen tread
Plunged into the lakes, sank or swam at will.

    Not all quietly fed upon the shrubs
And undisturbed lived peaceably,—for some
Of nature fierce, ferocious, when the night
Descended, from the brakes or dens came forth,
And walked the plains with glaring eyes, or crouched
Amid the thickets, or behind a ledge
Of rocks and suddenly devoured their prey.
The mighty lion, conscious of his strength,
Proudly majestic, either walks or leaps
And shakes the hills. Betimes with head uplift
His roar re-echoes from the mountain sides.
These and like, princes 'mong the evil spirits

Possessed and governed, taking pride in them,
Their strength and power to overcome their foes.
The spirits now in strifes were frequent, one
Against another through the beasts possessed,
Inciting one another to devour.
The bear, the tiger and the leopard fierce,
Whose eyes ever roll restless for attack,
Gnash their teeth upon their victims when afar,
And lurking in the tangled brush their near
Approach await. New insects numberless
Of every size and color crawled the earth.
The crafty serpent, noxious, now first seen,
Moved his repulsive length upon the ground,
The last to represent the reptile kind
Before produced, but more degraded still.
Some small and harmless, others venomous
And huge with many a labyrinthine fold.
Leviathan, sea monster huge lay writhed
In many folds, involved among the waves,
Unsightly, fierce, which voyagers desist
To look upon for dread and change their course,
Fearing more than the hidden shoals or rocks.

A new race of fish swam the running streams
And peopled every sea, luxurious food,
And beautiful to the eye their delicate
Fins and scales. Birds appeared now first
Produced, an order higher than the fowl
As seen the previous day :—the eagle, hawk,
And vulture keen of sight, most like the kind
Previous. But most were smaller, plumaged rich,
Of nature gentle, timid, voiced to charm
With melody the day and tedious night,
Destined as sweet companions for the good.
   The earth replenished with whatever walked,
Or crawled or swam or flew all lovely smiled,
Containing all the fruit of past and germ
Of what would future come, creation's crown.
The green that once the hill slopes and dales clothed
Gave place to trees and charming flowers and fruits.
Club mosses, rank and bristly, yielded place
To goodly trees expanding gracefully
Their foliaged boughs : for fern and calamite
Fruitless, which grew in thickets dense beside
The waters, lakes and in the marshy pools,

Sprang cereals and orchards flushed with fruit,
Which bounteously now our tables load,
And satisfy the heart of man and beast.

   Thus clearly spirit power in shade and light
During the epoch travelled o'er appears;
Where day succeeds the night when all seems lost;
And beauty dawns from dense deformity;
And pleasures pains succeed as life from death!
For Spirit Infinite in light prevails,
And blindly evil feeds and ministers
To good, as clouds give beauty to the light,
Reflect, and too make lovely setting sun!
O God! our God! how wonderful Thy power,
Thy holiness, Thy glory, O! how bright,
Thy perfect wisdom deep, unfathomable,
Thou dost alone the cravings of the mind—
The creature mind and heart fulfil and meet
And satisfy,—aught else creates unrest
And leaves a void which nature never fills!

BOOK VII.

CREATION OF MAN.

ALMIGHTY Elohim looked upon the world
And said, Let us now make man in our image,
In our own likeness: and let them have rule
Over the fish of sea and fowl of the air
And over cattle, every creeping thing
That creepeth on the ground and all the earth.
Then God created man both beautiful
And lovely: in the image like Himself
Him He made; male and female them created.
Then blessing by conferring blessings, said,
Be fruitful, multiply, replenish the earth
And subdue it: and have dominion over
Fish of the sea and fowl whose element
Is air and over every living thing
That moveth upon the face of all the earth.

Not necessarily full-grown when first
He came from the Almighty Maker's hand :—
A mammoth infant, ignorant, mature,—
With instinct less than brutes',—with senses, limbs
Entire, but knowing not the function, use
Or office of a single one,—an infant
In intellect and in his moral powers—
His smile e'en would betray an idiot—
With body full-grown coming into the world
And powerless !—this theory accepted
Is sheer credulity, unauthorized
By science, nor revealed by God to man.
Religious faith by fancies mythical
Is not sustained, but by the light of truth.
Science and nature see a prodigy,—
A monster birth, disrupting nature's womb
Maternal, violating sense and reason
In man mature, and born to earth full-grown !
Thus scepticism is helped, not overcome,
By faith more honest than intelligent.

  Earth offers nothing sweeter than a babe,—
So innocent and tender, chaste and pure

That scarcely we'll believe but heaven is robbed
Of cherubs from Elysian fields of bliss,
When they in earth appear and smile with love:
And angel pinions seem to fan the air,
And multitudes who guard their bed with care,
While gently sleeps the babe in arms of peace.
In feeble infancy the Living God
Unfolds in history His mighty plans.
Moses a lovely babe upon the Nile
And Christ a manger babe in Bethlehem
Of subsequent events are living germs.
'Tis thinkable that from a human germ,
Created new as other germs before,
Impregned in what is nearest kin to man
By Spirit Infinite, miraculous,
By God intervening, a lovely babe
At first was Adam; nurtured till mature;
Of God provided for:—for matter ne'er
Advanced one species higher than its kind;
And spirit finite knows no law,—desire
Has none a higher type to propagate
Other than its own.   This is nature's law

By revelation and experience known.
The highest type of life is powerless
Save only to use and in its normal use
To strengthen that with which it is endowed.
To advance from lower to a higher type
Is suicidal as the phœnix bird
Upon her nest in flames, her funeral pyre.
For man's regeneration spiritual
God's agency alone the Scriptures teach
Us is required—truth made prominent
In God's word: much more then for physical,
Since force in matter is through spirit solely,
And independent of the Infinite
At times, indeed, our spirit wills and acts.
E'en spirit ne'er regenerates itself:
Much more where matter is advanced above
Its kind, must Spirit act and do the work,
And Spirit Infinite, whose dwelling-place
And awful throne are hid from mortal view.
Thus Jesus in the virgin womb of Mary
By Spirit Power Divine, the Holy Ghost
O'ershadowing mortal flesh, became God's Son—

Beyond conception higher than earth's sons,
Yet of His mother nursed and taught, a babe
Helpless, subject to parents till mature!—
The highest revelation history
Records of earth and man. O! holy thought,
That Christ not only paves the way to Heaven,
But also rends the veil of mystery
Dividing past and future, showing how
Higher types of life into Being came,—
Not by laws natural, but Spirit Power!
His birth and death alike the mysteries
Of ages lay bare to intelligence.
God intervenes where nature's laws, ordained
Of Him, fail to accomplish His designs.
O! multiform the expression of Himself
He gives, infinite, in heaven and in earth!
Proud Rome, arraying lineage divine,
Claims for its founders Romulus and Remus,
Silvia's offspring by the god of war,
Their mother mortal, but their sire divine.
The legend also tells us that the babes
Weeping at the foot of Palatine Hill

The savage nature of a female wolf
Softened and moved to give them suck and rear
In her own cave, together with her young.
Not improbable, for in modern times,
Of recent date in Ind, in tropic climes
Two babes thus nurtured were until mature.
Thus legends, fables, myths of ancient lore
Become oftentimes the shadows of the truth.

    Adam of dust made, having life, became
With soul divine God's image manifest:
The lord of earth's domain, whose sovereign eye
Ferocious beasts induced to fawn beneath
His feet, subject to his will when mature.
So nobly formed, with limbs symmetrical,
Erect he moved majestic. Earth with pride
And swelling bosom heaved to feel his tread;
As throbs a maiden's guileless heart when first
She hears the voice of love from him for whom
Impatiently she yearns. His countenance beamed
Radiant and heavenly pure with smiles of bliss.

    Thus perfect formed, the noble flower of earth
Appeared,—last-born: the summary of all

Perfections of the previous life; in whom
The types prefiguring his coming were
Fulfilled and culminate: the end and aim
For which this temple grand, magnificent
Was building through unreckoned ages past.
    With man creation ceased—the finished work.
The mountains, continents and isles were fixed,
Immovable; their end and office knew;
The restless waters measured and their bounds
Assigned. All progress ceased and staid its march
In wondrous man, creation's perfect work
So far as earth was destined to reveal,
As flow the lucid streams of ruddy dawn
Into the splendors of meridian day.
    How beautiful is man! who apprehends,
In measure knows God as revealed in all
His works, where manifest His glory shines,—
In studying which his intellectual powers
Expand, and he becomes in brilliant thought
And high resolve and lofty flight more like
Divinity. A child of heaven, who looks
With longing hope for immortality;

Whose soul may break away from chains of sense,
Weigh anchor and exulting bear away
Into the ocean of immensity;
Whose fancy paints the rosy skies and flowers
In brighter tints, the verdant vales and hills
In richer green, and beautifies the real:
With reason too endowed, the highest gift
In exercise his spirit power possessed:
Whose sympathetic heart responds to all
The world without. The thunders deep and harsh,
And echoes of soft zephyrs 'mong the trees;
The music of the groves, the fountains, streams
And dales; the gloomy night and brilliant day
All find within the breast of man a chord
Responsive. Man accountable and free
Was too with will intelligent endowed;
A power to sink his soul in endless woe,
Or move beneath the rays of majesty
Divine, unveiled, and ever contemplate
God's glory and ethereal purity.
O! grave and awfully sacred was the trust!
With this no finite power in heaven or earth

Compares: a human gulf, both fathomless
Deep and wide—infinite to separate
Mankind and isolate him from the world!
Endless would be the task recounting all
The excellence and glory in which man
Upon creation shone,—transcending thought.

    To man thus formed was given every herb
Bearing seed upon the face of all the earth,
And every tree which yielded fruit for food.
And God complacently surveyed His work
And satisfied pronounced it very good.

    In the East, where blooming nature sweets produce
Of choicest kind for luxury to sense
Of sight and smell and taste, there Paradise
Was planted. And out of the ground God caused
To grow every tree pleasant to the sight
And good for food,—while in the midst the tree
Of life, whose fruit infused the soul with love
Of holiness and gave a heavenly joy
Which angels feel: and near by stood the tree

Bearing fruit of knowledge of good and evil,
As beautiful and proudly eminent.
    Eden high elevated, to view earth's
Expanse as lying at her feet and feel
The heavenly warmth of genial air, was rich
In scenery such as the eye ne'er since
Beheld: the mountain chains abrupt and high
In grand magnificence, and hills and plains
And valleys cool in shade meandered wild
And richly beautiful, as nature here
Was prodigal of her exhaustless wealth.
From Eden's blissful plains, as from a throne
Of bliss, a river flowed to irrigate
The fertile soil and parted into four
Streams; the first Pison whose impetuous flow
Cut gorges deep and rushed in headlong speed
Around the land of Havilah, where gold
And palms and fragrant gum and onyx stone
Abound, thence lost into the Caspian Sea;
The second Gihon foamed with angry roar
Through narrow mountain gorges and down steep
Precipices, and encompassed the whole

Land of Cush; next is Hiddekel which goeth
Toward the east of Assyria and now joins
The fourth, Euphrates, which together flow
Into the Persian Gulf far at the south.

    There might be heard the low and sullen moan
Of waves upon the north and east and south,
Contrasting with their own sweet melody
Of sparkling rills and fountains, and there seen
The tranquil plains and smooth unbroken downs
Extended far in the west, in glory crowned
Pre-eminent:—a throne that reached the clouds
Whence came the crystal streams, diverse their course,
And watered ridges, terraces and plains
Till where the horizon drew its curtain round
The earth—a habitation where the Lord
Appeared at times and angels loved to linger.

    Beneath the shade of cedars, towering oaks
And branching elms, and all the sylvan trees
Of goodly growth, flocks sportive played in wild
And happy glee without the thought of harm.
Gentle lambs skipped upon the meadows green,
And kid upon the steep and rugged rocks,

While sweet gazelles about the fountains clear
Frisking romped in their modest kindly way.
Here animals of nature fierce and wild
Dared not intrude; or if an entrance found
Their vengeful eye to soft expression changed.
Among the thickly woven branches, close
Entwined, in happy unison all kind
Of animals of gleesome nature played.
In the waters 'mong the golden sand and pearl,
And from beneath and round green mossy rocks
Darted fish, whose scales colored rich and rare
Gave forth a lustre changed at every turn.
How sweetly reigned repose and peace and joy
Within this pleasant garden—Heaven on earth!

    This happy seat was given into the hands
Of man to dress and keep and beautify,—
Worthy his care and he a worthy lord.
His princely form, his full reflective eye,
His high and noble brow with thought profound,
His every move and look, an energy—
A conquering power which nature dreads to dare,
Sincerity and truth and faith combined

With holiness and other qualities
Revealed the image of his Maker, God.
    Yet independence absolute, to act
His will with sovereign pleasure, was withheld
By God who formed him from the dust,—whose voice
Declared His own supremacy in tones
Of thunder as devouring fire, which shook
The earth and heaven :—Of every tree thou mayest
Freely eat save the fruit borne by the tree
Of knowledge of both good and evil, which
Shall not be eaten : for in the day thou eatest
Thereof thou'lt surely die. The sole command
Thus given resounded through the heavenly courts
And angels heard ; and darkness covered all
The earth, which sank beneath the penalty
As when an earthquake rocks a continent :
So nature long after gave signs of woe
When Christ in agony cried upon the cross !—
Eli, eli, lama sabachthani !
And Israel at Mount Sinai, hearing God's
Voice, saw the mountain quake and flames burst forth
And the earth tremble at their feet, as waves

Of troubled ocean when by tempests riven,—
And Israel greatly fearing sought the feet
Of Moses and entreated that the voice
Should not again address them, lést they die!
Adam with reverence heard and resolved
To keep the solemn trust inviolate.

'Twas fitting Adam's body made of dust,
Or elements which constitute the earth,
Should subject be to Spirit Power, Supreme—
Like earth itself; his spirit too submiss,
And recognize Creative glory—high
Enthroned above himself and all the earth.
The interdicted tree thenceforth became
A voice proclaiming to him—reverence!—
A heavenly voice; its solemn accents love;
Obeyed—the cadences were alway sweet,
Like nature's laws when madly not infringed.

Then before Adam were brought every beast
Of the field and all cattle and the fowl
Of heaven; and Adam named them as they passed
According to their nature and their kind.

When angels pure, in human form, were absent

Creation of Man.

He lonely seemed: no sweet communion found
With any living form that met his eye.
To his voice no response in answer came
From kindred heart.   Alone in revery
He'd wander happy in his innocence.
During the day beside the fountains sit
And muse upon their beauty and the life
Within, or ramble through the fragrant bowers
Reflecting how perfect was every plant
And flower: by night beneath the canopy
Of heaven, in silent awe he'd contemplate
The eternal splendor of the starry hosts.
The soothing glow of love unkindled lay
Dormant within his breast.   'Twas thus not long.
Heaven loved too well earth's perfect, chosen son.
Upon a time as was his wont, embowered
By asphodels and hyacinths, and fanned
By the cool, fragrant gale of sweets in Eden,
And asleep, God from his throbbing side took
Wherewith to form a woman for his love,—
To kindle in his nature passions new,
Ecstatic, most akin to those of heaven.

Long nursed by angels, hid from man or beast
Or fiend, fed upon ambrosial meats,
She grew in beauty, grace and charm akin
To cherub angels from elysian plains,
Who lovingly protected her from ill.
Ere long mature she was to Adam brought.
Her fair skin like the lilies in the streams
Of Paradise shed forth a lustre soft
As the first blush of morn ; her tresses hung
In wild luxuriance round her shoulders, decked
With choicest flowers, which winds in dalliance moved
And whispered in their happy sportful play
The while as fairies 'mong the tender herbs ;
With head reclining, in her heaving breast
Humility was marked in every move
And look, submission and a sweet reserve,—
Veiling but most revealed the hidden worth ;
Naked though not ashamed, for innocent.
Adam embraced his tender bride and felt
Himself a gushing fountain full of love—
A new delight which rendered Eden Heaven.
Now heaven's best gift was first revealed to earth.

Love! heaven's light; an attribute of God;
More sweet than aught else; pure, immortal fire;
Which angels share and have in eminence,—
Exceeding beautiful, undimmed by sin;
Which lights this gloomy vale—this vale of tears,
Transforming earth to heaven, when bright it shines
And pure within our sacred shrine, the heart!
Paradise seemed a desert waste apart
From her whose tenderness, simplicity
And every womanly charm, radiant shed
Peculiar lustre and grace in their sweet
Abode. Naught here was wanting to complete
Their bliss unalloyed, overflowing full.

    The lovely pair at times walked 'mong the fig,
Citron and almond trees, and plucked the fruit
Delicious hanging upon the bended boughs
Inviting them indulgent to repast;
Or half reclined upon a downy bed
Of violets beside the streams of Eden
And talked of love. While swans before them played
Upon the glassy waters; and birds sang
In chorus songs of thrilling ecstasy;

And bees in myriads hummed among the flowers
And blossomed fruit trees, diligently sipped
Their nectar sweet; and butterflies, whose wings
With iris tinged and dust of gold, begemmed
The air.   Then all creation echoed love
Within the gates of Eden, their sweet realm.
When glowed the West with red, and evening shades
Drew on, retired within their garnished bower,
The nightingales enchanting notes of soft
And wild and warbling melody would lull
Them to repose : a rest, which innocent,
They only knew—to mankind since denied !
Undisturbed by dire grief, which oft in sleep
Beat us as waves upon a rocky coast,
The happy pair reposed in quietude,
As lakes of Paradise translucent slept
In the arms of their smiling shores.   Their bed,
Of violet flowers perfumed with spikenard, myrrh
And frankincense; their canopy, the vault
Cerulean, as 'twere curtains scarlet rich,
Adorned with stars, seemed stooping low to hide

And shield them from the world, whose diadem
They were, creation's crown and set with gems.

    All nature, every animal and man
Within the gates of Eden's realm, were good
And true and beautiful—for former things
Had passed away,—by Spirit Power subdued:
A prophecy of heaven and earth reclaimed
When this our present period shall end.
Without the realm of happy Eden all
The powers of darkness were as fierce, malign
And evil as before: a truth adverse,
A prophecy against the theories
Which claim that sin will be in time extinct,
Like reptiles of a pre-historic age;
That God cannot, in virtue of His love,
Forbear to save all, both in earth and hell!
Fain we'd endorse did Scripture teach the view,
Or reason even, divorced from sentiment.
Vain trust for license to indulge in sin!
Sin ne'er extinguishes the spirit life,
Like luminaries once in heaven whose fires

Are quenched; and God nowhere encourages
Belief, that hell shall ultimately cease,
But solemnly we're taught the opposite.
Like wanton boys in chase of baubles, bright
To eye of sense, men trifle thus with God
Or heaven or hell, for all eternity!

   From heaven to Eden in shining myriads
The angels pure and sweet now visited
The happy human pair: for harmony
Prevailed—peace reigned in blissful Paradise
Subject to heaven's light and purity.
A beauteous halo of the heavenly world
Illumed their brow; a smile so gentle, meek
And kind that every hidden spring of love
In man or angel was unsealed thereby:
Untarnished by the blighting touch of sin:
Whose beauty shone with lustre unimpaired
By years, and virtue with no weakness charged.
Adoring worshippers, who contemplate
The Deity's perfections as revealed,—
Who've ever dwelt where truth and beauty reigns,—

Where universal knowledge is disclosed,—
Where mysteries for ages hid are searched
Out and continually are unsealed.
Most beauteously they reflect the grace
Of love, which in an infinite degree
Abides within the heart of Deity,—
A feature that endears, pre-eminent
In heaven—the virtue of their spirit pure.
   'Tis here spirit finite, in normal state,
Its highest excellence and grace attains,—
Is lovely as the glowing light of heaven,—
As beautiful as glows a maiden's cheek,—
As sweet as flowers when wet with morning dews,—
And ravishing in all that render heaven
A Paradise for joy and bliss ecstatic:
Attains to power for thought as days give place
To years, and years to all eternity,
Becoming nigher like God, infinite—
But ever humble, ne'er in lust for power,
Unconscious, seemingly, of excellence!
   From lofty eminences in their realm
Angels viewed earth and Paradise and man.

As ne'er before the fountain of their love
Was moved for man; with them co-heir of heaven
And bliss and glory.   Paradise revealed
A glory new and unsurpassed in heaven—
Evil subdued and life produced from death.
From heaven solely came such wealth of love
As now in angel bosoms yearned for man.
Nor unrequited were the angels; Adam
And Eve gave quick response in sympathy
And accord with their heavenly visitants.
Such harmony as quivered through the realm
Of Eden, and love that moved the human soul
And angels, earth ne'er since has known or felt.

BOOK VIII.

MAN'S FALL.

ALAS! that man should barter Paradise
For woe and death: and not he suffer solely,
But should entail the same upon the race,—
Else holy, innocent and happy still.
The human pair could eat the fruit of life,
And thus preclude the withering and cold chill
Of death, and live in holiness forever,—
Had they withstood temptation as did Christ,
Our Lord, for forty days and nights assailed:
For of the tree of knowledge of both good
And evil God forbade them taste or touch.
Thus narrow is the road dividing life
From death: the way enticing too. All seems
Pleasant and fair along that highway, paved

With flowers and cooled with arborescent trees,—
But 'tis the way of death ! Upon this tree
Grew fruit whose touch both soul and body poisoned,
Though good for food and pleasant to behold,—
Because forbidden them of God, Supreme.
In Eden it grew nigh the tree of life.
The way dividing life from death's abyss
Is easily crossed by man's or hell's device.

    The serpent subtily an entrance found
In Eden, unbeknown to man or angel,
Guided by Satan, a fit habitat
For the hostile enemy of God and man,
Which the Devil led to tempt with fair words
The destined mother of the human race ;
And taught its forked and fiery tongue to speak
His hellish thoughts respecting God's command
In words of scorn, which led Eve to transgress.
For scorn disarms the soul of fear and love,
Subjects the tempted to the tempter's wiles.
With such infernal art the Devil, Eve
Addressed, his suit won, the end of which was death.
Yea ! hath God said, ye shall not eat the fruit

Of every tree that in the garden grows?—
The subtle serpent scornfully inquired.
    The woman meekly answering said, The fruit
Of every tree we may with freedom eat,
Save that of good and evil, which alone
God forbade us eat or touch lest we die.
    The artful tempter, knowing well the heart
Of woman, innocent and credulous,
Filled her breast with ambitious themes, unthought
Before, the source of woe, from whence have flown
The streams which deluge earth with woe and
    death!
Ye shall not surely die: for God doth know
That in the day ye eat thereof your eyes
Shall open and ye shall with clearness see
Both good and evil, then shall be as gods,
Exalted 'bove your present state, and range
The heavens whence angels come as swift as light,—
The Devil answered, charging first a lie
Upon the Infinite and holy God,
And after, with ambitious schemes he filled
The breast, as pure as snow, of lovely Eve!

The heartless Tempter, bent on naught but ill,
The Serpent, now had done his wicked work.

.Modern philosophy when questioning
Whether it was an actual reptile used
Nothing gains.   Scriptures simplify the truth.
'Tis not improbable the beast by Satan
Was fashioned,—certainly 'twas suitable
For him to lead and compass his designs.
An ass a wicked prophet once rebuked
Through spirit not her own, controlled thereby.
Our tongues are mute not moved by spirit power,
Which may another's be and not our own.
Christ His disciples taught dependence upon
Himself, when they to answer cavilling kings
Were called, instructing them, 'Tis I that speak.
The form of matter used by spirit power
To act for good or evil signifies
Little and is quite immaterial.
Philosophy is rendering itself
Ridiculous, is pusillanimous,
Is in her dotage state, or run to seed,

Man's Fall.

When cavilling about a serpent used
For speech by spirit power. Will please the savans
Answer, How comes their tongues, of matter pure,
To speak their cavilling thoughts and vain conceits?

   Ambitious, lofty aims then first possessed
Eve's mind, made discontented with her lot
Of meek subjection to the higher powers:
Forgetting that her sphere was that of love
And purity,—a sweet ethereal power
Of equal weight against a conquering grasp
Of thought, subjecting elemental force,
And delving deep in hidden mystery.
Oft had she drank of wisdom's fount which flowed
All pure and lucid from the noble soul
Of Adam, while she in his bosom lay,
And nestled there a gentle dove, and cooled
His brow with her hand delicately white
As lilies which in Eden's fountains grew.
Oft had she all lovingly watched the glow
Of ardent zeal that burned his cheek and fired
His eye, and listened to his words of power

Refreshing to her soul like summer showers
Upon a thirsty soil. She to inquire,—
He to instruct,—and amply paid his zeal
If but he heard her music voice approve,—
She to react and soften his manly powers,
Were formed—each noble in their sphere alike.
The tempter by his artful words induced
Lovely Eve to forego her sweet dominion
Over man and filled her soul with new thoughts,
Ambitious aspirations, far beyond
The appointed end for which made by the hand
Divine. So now with other eyes than erst
She looked upon the fatal tree, her soul
Already poisoned by the serpent's guile.
Behold the fruit was luscious, good for food,
Of scent that sharpened keen the appetite ;
And pleasant to the eye, of yellow tint
And reddish glow ; but last of all, a fruit
Desirable to make one wise. This thought
Prevailed ; the moving cause her love for Adam
Possibly ;—thinking she'd to him impart
Surprising wisdom, hidden hitherto,

And please and emulate her noble lord.
In her simplicity she credited
The subtle, lying words by Satan spoken,
Or else forgetful of the doom imposed,
Or drowning for the time the warning voice
Within, most rashly plucked the fruit and ate!

 The angels one and all from Paradise
Took flight at once, amazed but sorrowful
As ne'er before, and entering heaven's realm,
A mighty host, with faces veiled beneath
Their wings, in broken sighs the news conveyed!
 The deed was done—that chilled the universe
Like death! in heaven the angels' countenances fell:
They dropt their golden harps,—all music ceased—
And silence reigned: for there the spirits pure
Who kept their first estate, watched long in dread
Suspense God's new created work, upright
Man, wondering if he'd stand or grossly fall.
They knew that God offended was a fire
Devouring: saw the awful penalty
Inflicted upon the rebel spirits, once

As pure as they, their brethren and their kin.
Was man so lovely, for whom their souls yearned
With pure affection, strong as angels feel,
Destined to undergo like doom; to be
Transformed to devils vile, and chained with chains
Of adamant, confined to sulphurous waves
Which bellow harshly and shriek through the depths
Infernal; earth lose its sweetness, formed
In vain,—the charnel-house of woe in place
Of joy? One cherished hope alone was left:
Adam was uninformed as yet by Eve
Of the crime she'd done, and untempted stood
Alone in holiness. The angels paused
Expectant, hopeful that all was not lost.

    Not long uncertain: Eve was tempter now,
Divinely formed with every winning grace,
And no marvel if Adam was her slave,
Devoted, alway yielding to her suit
With quick assent. Not easy to entice
Would Adam pure have been in Satan's hands.
But Eve the tempter, though his judgment, heart
And conscience disapproved, her loving smile

And plea and sweet caresses to resist
Was humanly, though pure, beyond his power.
With her to suffer all the penalty
And die, if die they must, was preferable
To having Eve endure alone the sting!

   Thus reasoned love, and from her hand he took
The baneful fruit, all fair without, and he
With her did eat. All now was over. Hell's
Discordant jubilee rolled grimly round
The throne of light and power where sat the King
Eternal. Heaven was mournful sad—in gloom!
The angels closed their eyes, and bowing hid
Their radiant faces in their hands—and wept!

   So closed the solemn drama, whose sad gloom
Invaded for a second time heaven's light,
And palled the universe. The eyes of both
Were opened and they saw—their nakedness.
Eve erst, all happy, holy, innocent,
Pure as the lily white was now condemned,
Both soul and body to death temporal
And death eternal ere the voice of God

Was heard: and Adam of unrivalled power
And excellence with her like doomed. Their crown
They forfeited by sin; the deed their own.
Tempted they aimed at independence, wished
Like Satan, who first against heaven conspired,
To be like gods, and vile like Satan grew,—
With hell's fierce fire just kindled in the soul.

    Alas! how changed the temple, so adorned
And brilliant, noble, perfect to reflect
Divinely the image of their Maker God!
But desolate its ruins—by sin laid waste,
Which solely mars or utterly destroys,
And since has filled the earth with groans and blood!

    Now gloom, palled of hell, settled heavily
Upon the world; and sepulchres of death
And horrid powers were opened and laid bare
In earth. An ancient night of chaos seemed
About to add a realm to hell's domain.

    Separate by transgression from the source
Of life, the spirit shattered drifts away
From God, His hand not on the helm, with sails

Full spread before the ever-veering gale.
The evil passions, selfishness, deceit,
Resentment, hate and all that from corrupt
Nature flow gain firm hold upon the soul
Debased, depraved,—the understanding dark,—
Blind to the beauteous light of holiness:
Bound firmly in bonds of iniquity,
The chains of more than adamantine strength:
The conscience overpowered by evil lusts,
Impaired by every new offence, until
Its tender, sweetest tones, are indistinct:
Its spirit power impaired for good;—for evil
Rendered more vigorous by length of time
And practice in the ways of sin. No power
Annihilates the soul, or can except
Omnific and Divine, which gave it being.
No suicide of soul in earth or hell
By any seeking death is possible.
O! could the dense, dark veil of mystery
Be lifted from the spirit world, and light
From the empyrean heights shine upon the depths
And for a moment fallen spirit self

Behold, debased in all its moral power,
Its true estate compared to holiness
Conceive,—aghast and shrieking it would seek
Sulphurous hell congenial for relief!

    To charge the holy God with sin, because
Forsooth the human pair and angels fell,
Is sacrilege by fools without the worth
Of effort to reclaim,—who're past the power
Of thought, the light of reason or of truth!
The guilt was man's. A covenant for life
He broke, which for his happiness heaven made.
Rash man perverted what was done in love:
If God His creatures with a silken cord
Thus chose to bind for good, to quicken faith
In Him, their highest good, who can dispute
His love; and to condemn, as lawful judge,
If man from unbelief transgressed? For faith
Absent, man is in league with hell no less
When first he fell in Eden than now! The dread
Fiend death firmly on the soul had seized,
Which with his horrid rule he swayed, as God
Forewarned, the moment man partook the fruit

Forbidden : for all communion with the source
Of moral excellence ceased, which is life.
Immortal man by disobedience steeped
In moral guilt and vile impurity
Was lost alas ! for all eternity !

    In novelistic attitude and mien
Some modern churches cry for charity,
For sentimentalism and fictious tales ;
For soft and sweet words to state startling truths ;
For lavender religion oiled with sweets
To gratify the sense, though spirit starve
And die,—in soporific state prefer
To dream rather than be brought into action
By statements clear of what the Scriptures teach :
And thus awake, alas ! as Dives waked
In hell, confused, amazed, from torpor self
Imposed, to face an awful doom eternal !
Their clergy yield for bread, and meekly ask
In pious accents, Why the lethargy
In church and evil rampant in the world ?
If any nobly stand to vindicate

The truth—less keen to what is popular
Than honest in what Heaven ordains to teach,—
They're deemed imprudent, reckless and unwise
By patronage men, who're wise weathercocks
To steepled churches, falsely pastors called.
Such pastors not alone at fault, though shame,
Confusion and remorse belong to them
For cowardice and sacred trust betrayed;
But clamorous for sentiment their churches
Crave novelty, and light and frivolous
Antics to please imaginative sense,
The eye or ear; prefer the sacred desk
Adorned with blossom-youth, and tender, bright
And jovial, upon the fashions posted—
Not over-freighted with theology,
And loathe the fruit which long experience
Has well matured in beauty, age and grace!
By elders e'en the inexperienced
Are placed above the agéd, wise and good,
And deemed both eminent and fit to lead—
And so the youths esteem and think themselves!
'Tis then that every boy or boor prefers

Himself a candidate for churchly office—
Where ignorance is equal to conceit,—
Good cobblers spoiled in making poor divines!
Such churches blossom ask, on blossom starve,—
And shame the blesséd cause espoused by them,—
Forgetting God Supreme, relying most
Upon fertility untried of genius
Supposed or claimed, which may produce pure grain,
Or may but yield prolific noxious weeds.
Religious thought, discourse mature, condensed
Is deemed infliction rude, unkind by brain
Too giddy save to be adorned with flowers,
With heart insensible and dull and cold—
Spirit power, alas! quenched in opiates,—
For neither good nor evil capable
To any great or serious extent.
Themselves they wrong more than afflict their kind.
Alas! that spirits like to God should sport
Themselves—mere birds or butterflies adorned
With gaudy wings to glitter for a day,—
And die for lack of food where plenty reigns!
 Jesus! who to the infant Church didst send

Thy blesséd Spirit, Comforter Divine,
To fire with heat celestial and revive
Its drooping faith, oh, lead our wandering feet
From haunts of gayety and stifling airs
And worldly indolence, in pastures green,
Amid the olive groves with Thee to watch
And pray, or in the mountain solitudes—
In spirit to behold Thee in Thy home
From clear and heavenly atmospheres, most blessed!
'Twas wrath Divine against appalling sins
That agonize the world, which caused Thy soul,
O, dearest Lord! to agonize for us,
With prayers and burning words in Olive's shade;
Which bowed Thee as a feeble thing to earth;
Which sickened Thee to bleed at every pore;
Which forced dark waters, supernatural gloom,
And dread of death and fear of wrath Divine
To overwhelm Thy pure, transparent soul;
Which caused beneath the heavy load Thy head
To droop and sink, deathlike upon Thy breast!
And now, O! horrible to think! shall man—
For whom such sacrifice is made, deem sin

But light and trivial, a little cloud
Perchance that will soon disappear, a web
That can but easily be brushed away?
Shall man deem service in the church a light
And easy thing, and smile a sunshine day
And night, and breathe an air perfumed, and walk
With head upon one shoulder set,—nor heed
Gethsemane, nor God's blood, shed for sin!
Oh, that with holy fear, and conscience cleansed,
Beneath the shade and in the midnight hours,
Oh, Saviour dear, Thy servants might abide
With Thee, and see the load which Thou didst
    bear,—
And weep in sorrow, pain and grief with Thee!

    Justice exacts the penalty of sin, .
Rendered imperative by holiness.
And pleading ne'er can purify a soul!
God being just and holy must inflict
Sin's penalty upon a soul corrupt.
Nay, too! the conscience stings aside from God
And unrelentingly, eternally!

Our conscience ne'er relents e'en when it feels
The victim nigh the gates of hell shrink back
With horror, cold with dread remorse ; nor when
The eager fiends seize upon the soul,
Which struggles fruitlessly within their grasp !
A guilty soul could not inhabit heaven,
Where purity and sweets alone abide !
In earth the conscience unrelentingly
Inflicts the penalty which sin exacts,—
Much more when earth's attractions are removed.
To cavil and demand a milder sentence
Is quarrelling with what is natural,
Ourselves as made, our soul, our native powers,
Aside from judgment visited by heaven
And holy God direct and merited.
Yet God is not in suffering we endure,
Nor we in God when cut adrift by sin.

    Tremendous deed ! man broke the golden link
That bound him to the throne of bliss and heaven.
No sadder thought than from an amplitude
Of bliss man plunged into a fathomless
Abyss of woe !   No human grasp of thought

Man's Fall.

Or sense or feeling can portray the deep,
Enormous guilt of moral turpitude!
   Thus earth's exquisite temple was in ruins;
And strife in eminence enthroned; and man
In whom all nature's treasured gems shone forth,
The focus where converged was all the light
Of bygone ages, was now ruined, fallen
And shattered in his overthrow—all waste.
He wronged his own soul, God-like and divine!

   The Dragon and his black ferocious brood
Had now a subject worthy of their skill,
Upon whom to practice cunning subtlety
And hellish arts, far in advance of beasts
Noxious which pre-historic they'd possessed,—
And capable of studied arts, refined
To agonize with torture most intense
And varied victims whom they'd undertake
To follow were it possible beyond
The grave, and render hell aglee by deeds
Beyond its daring heaven's wrath hitherto!
When man was made in image like to God

And Eden planted, heaven then raised her throne
Upon the earth and hell had lost her realm,—
Within the province of Beelzebub
War had been carried and a victory
Gained.　But now hell is victor, heaven in
　　　gloom—
The first victory gained by Satan's wiles.
No heavenly messenger on earth, it seemed
Consigned to him alone, and solely hell's
Domain.　No wonder courage now resumed
Its potent sway in every fiend breast;
And a grand jubilee, discordant, fierce,
Malign, in honor of the event was held.
The evil spirits had increased in lust
Of horrid sins, had mostly lost the marks
Of their once holy state of purity,—
But no decrease of power though misapplied.
'Twas now their pleasure to defy the powers
Of heaven; to wallow in the sinks of sin;
To relish seeing others' misery;
To do whate'er is foul, the antipodes
Of all that's good and pleasing to the pure,—

The heights whence fallen, determining the depths
They'd reached and active power in doing evil.
    Their jubilee! was hell resuming sway
More potent over elemental powers,
The earth and sea and air, the winds and clouds.
Long chained in hell's abyss they'd been, because
Evil had been in measure limited
By Eden's peaceful reign and man created
Holy—in place of death life substituted.
Now unchained, being free to range the earth,
Inflated by success, they recognized
The power of evil, vainly thought themselves
Sufficient to assault and conquer heaven!
Nothing gives promise of success more than
Success; and lifts the head, and air imparts
Of self-conceit and conscious self-importance,
Gaited in moves and patronizing words,—
E'en when success is gained unmerited.
This weakness renders Devils ludicrous,—
But earth out-herods Herod's vanity.
When men strut with face lifted to the stars,
And tread the ground with dainty feet and legs

As springs, then hell is filled with merriment,
And shouts of laughter ring through her dun air!
    The Scriptures tell us that Elisha's servant,
Fearing the Syrian enemies surrounding
Dothan, was given, through Elisha's prayer,
To see the mountains full of heaven's heroes,
With fire and horse, to guard and shield and save
The prophet; company innumerable,
A strong celestial host, then thousand times
Ten thousand, forces called God's chariots.
Thus were earth's mountains, plains, and seas and air,
Now filled with fiends foul, apostates freed
From Stygian lakes. Black clouds obscured the earth,
Except when lurid lightnings warred with heaven's
Artillery; the waves of every sea
Dashed angrily and high upon the shores;
Earthquakes rocked and rent every continent;
Volcanoes heaved their liquid fires above
The clouds; earth quivered to her central zones!
Fear palled and trembling shook the human pair.
Tumult on earth whichever way they looked,
And ruin everywhere—th' empyrean heights

Of heaven above the clouds alone serene.
Reptiles and crocodiles their native streams
And ponds deserted for the lands and groves,
And serpents huge of seas in terror sought
The shores. No creature having life and breath
But sought to hide, not knowing where to flee!*

When subsequently, after centuries,
Jesus, earth's Lord and Saviour, conquered hell
Upon the Cross, and yielded up the ghost,
Then also in like manner earth gave signs
Of woe in sympathy with heaven foiled
And conquered, as to it appeared, by hell
A second time. Then holy angels too

---

* The traveller Humboldt tells us, after witnessing an earthquake in South America, even the crocodiles ran from the River Orinoco, howling into the woods, the dogs and pigs were powerless with fear. The whole city seemed "the hearth of destruction." The houses could not shelter, for they were falling in ruins. He turned to the trees, but they were overthrown. His next thought was to run to the mountains, but they were reeling like drunken men. He then looked toward the sea. Lo! it had fled; and the ships, which a few moments before were in deep water, were rocking on the bare sand. He tells us that being then at his wits' end, he looked up and observed that heaven alone was calm and unshaken.

In air with groans and sighs from clouds above,
Addressed a navigator sailing through
The Adrian seas, alarming all the crew,
In words they little understood, in tones
Of thunder:—When Palodes is reached, publish,—
'Ο μεγας Παν τεθνηκε ! * Calm upon
The sea their purpose foiled to disobey
The heavenly voice when Palodes was reached.
Then Thamus seeing heaven's intent again,
Announced what sounded strange to every ear,
Nor understood. When Jesus suffered death
Hell victor seemed as first when man transgressed.
Hence Heaven to vindicate, He in a body
Spiritual entered Hades from the Cross
At once; subdued the armaments prepared
To overrun the earth and crush the race
Of man; in spirit-body preached to spirits
Which were before the flood in prison chained;
Confirming prophecy to their remorse;
Showing in flesh He had to do with man,
In spirit with the spirits of the dead—

* "*The great God Pan is dead!*" Plutarch's Defect of Oracles.

Was still Supreme in heaven and earth and hell;
Showing that hell's apparent victory
Was its most fatal and inglorious
Defeat; that, though His flesh might be destroyed
His Godhead spirit would assert itself,
Its power, in spirit-body like their own—
Save that with light He shone, they like the night,—
To vex and punish them if not submiss
To will divine, more potent than in flesh.
'Twas needful,—hell was jubilant,—its powers
Infernal, having failed to tempt, had moved
Vile men to crucify the Son of God!
Their power, if not restrained, would render earth
A hell in fact and sinful man more vile
Than they, more dangerous, corrupt and cruel.
'Twas seen in their possessing man and beast
When given liberty, while Christ sojourned
Below, then wholly subject to His power.
Since God atoned for sin to save the earth,
E'en through infernal powers, the instruments—
The schemes of hell recoiling 'gainst itself,
'Twas fitting now that Christ should enter hell

In might divine and chain the powers of evil,
Restrain their liberty in large degree,
And close the gates of their deep, dark abyss
Upon a multitude which hitherto
Had ranged the earth, tormented men, and sought
To overcome God manifest in flesh.
Hence while reflecting upon His death and near
The Cross and finished work, He clearly said:—
Now is the world judged and its prince cast out.
Yet liberty to many Heaven allows,
For wise and righteous ends to be revealed.

    Hell breathless feared beneath His righteous tread;
And shrank aghast before His searching eye;
And shook and trembled like a mighty oak
Before a blast, when listening to His voice.
They'd never seen the form of God in spirit
Nature, as theirs, whose power they'd always felt!
He went to them,—He showed Himself alive,—
He preached—but not the gospel news of peace,—
Appeared their victor and their righteous Lord.
As Noah's preaching, tears and warning voice
Had been despised, and his despisers perished,—

'Twas fitting Christ despised and put to death
Should go to them, and teach through them the powers
Of hell, that judgment surely follows sin.
His entering hell was judgment in itself
Upon the fiends who'd battled for the world.
As righteous Noah judgment prophesied,
So Christ, the antitype, in Hades preached
A second judgment upon the spirits foul,
Who'd their own selves defeated more than Heaven
By compassing through man His cruel death,—
As always guilty men afflict themselves
By crimes their own, which never fail to sting
Themselves, more than the righteous innocent—
For sinners are unconscious suicides :—
The second judgment in severity
To be determined by their future guilt!
Then doubtless spirits obdurate and fierce
From His own lips heard and expect the day,
When earth will be a paradise reclaimed,
And peace be conquered here by Spirit Power.

    Hence Christ in Hades preaching, no hope gives
That finally hell's lost will be reclaimed

By satisfaction made for sin on earth.
For simply heaven's Son asserted power
Immaculate, and reaped the precious fruits
Of victory for earth and sons redeemed.

Upon the fall of man they little knew
The mind or purpose of the Invisible.
Hence were the fiends at the time of Christ,
And more especially before, and most
Before the flood malignant, active, vile—
But alway wicked, active and malign
Enough to fill the earth with groans, and sink
Unwary, yielding souls into perdition;—
But active most where good is being done—
No need where wickedness prevails, and men
Already are their willing votaries.

The evil spirit feast of jubilee
And revelry had every fallen angel
Convoked from every prison cell or cave
Or grotto, cavern or abyss throughout
Their habitations far and near, in earth

Man's Fall.

Or planets in the universe entire.
Long time they gloated in confusion's reign;
In seething fires, or lurid flames, or earth's
Dun air held carnival; till 'gain aroused
By Spirit Power, displayed anew and strange.

    This last, the seventh day, remains unsung,
Which with alternate light and shade appears,
In gloom and light, in pain and happiness,—
Which dawned with man's appearing on the earth
And ends with paradise, more beauteous,
Restored to man, with bliss unknown before,
And Man exalted to the throne of heaven!

BOOK IX.

MAN REDEEMED.

In Genesis the days commence with evening
And end with morning, with some new advance,
Given of Spirit Power in exercise—
Development from lower to the higher
Stages, which we've endeavored to portray:
Each day a period whose length of time
We neither know nor need to care to know,
A fact in abstract quite immaterial:
Notable, too, that Scripture language all
The days, in number six, embraced in one
In words thus,—These the generations are
Of heavens and earth created, in *the day*
The Lord God made the earth and the heavens.
The Scriptures for the seventh day—a fact

To be observed—records no evening to
Commence the day, as for the others all,
Nor morning terminating it as others.
The order of the past is now reversed
For this the seventh day or period,
Commenced when morning dawned most beauteous
With man and ends with earth destroyed by fire—
A fact revealed to us by prophecy:
A period continuous until
The heavens shall roll together as a scroll,
The elements shall melt with fervent heat,
The sun be turned to darkness and the moon
Into blood, and a new heaven and new earth
Appear, and spiritual like the body
Renewed,—when time shall pass away, be lost
Into eternity. In confirmation
Of prophecy astounded we've beheld
Other worlds blaze with more than wonted light,
Then slowly disappear—ranked 'mong lost stars:
As that nigh Cassiopia which kindled bright
As Sirius, then began to fade and soon
Totally vanished, lost to the universe

Of worlds ; or that nigh Altair rivalling
In brilliancy e'en our sweet evening star ;
Or one that decked Orion's lustrous group ;
Or Scorpion's no longer lighting heaven.
Significant fact ! wingéd messengers
Of death and dissolution from the depths
Of space confirming God's inspired word.
To such a final doom the earth through time
Immeasurable has steadily progressed.

When finally shall end the era sixth,
The last of earth, now reached and far advanced,
Then shall begin the seventh period :—
From conflicting elements will appear
The earth anew and heavens luminous
With light :—creation from the curse released
Will then rejoice in winter past and gone ;
In storms then o'er, the chilling blasts, the snow,
The hail ; no thunder peals to rend the sky
Serene, nor dense clouds to o'ershadow heaven :
For spring forever fresh will never cease.
The nightingale and cooing turtle-dove
Will sing as ne'er before their notes of love.

The vale of tears, bereavements, deaths belong
To earth as once, but ne'er to reappear!
   'Tis marvellous how history repeats
Itself; how simple truths original
Are, found when correspondence is observed
Between the facts past, present and to come.
As there are six distinct creative days
Embraced in one creative period,—
So we'll observe, and wondering adore
Omniscience, that there are redemptive days,
Notable by some epoch or event
Commencing and ending a period :
The number six of eras most distinct,
And all embraced in one redemptive day,
The day for gladdened jubilee, when God
Had ended all His works which He had made.
In it embraced are all the previous germs
Which in their day developed and decayed ;
But far advanced is this since conscience reigns,—
Superinduced supreme in spirit life.
This the hallowed Sabbath for man to advance
In holiness, attain a happier seat,

Drink fuller than the joys of Paradise.
Fallen man redeemed and glorified to sit
In heavenly places with the atoning Lamb
Of God, oh, who'd dare venture such a thought,
Were't not revealed to man in Holy Writ—
A vision beatific of heaven's rest!

    Hence unity organic here prevails,
Development controlled by Spirit Power,
And energized as in creative work:
One thought and purpose running through the whole;
One scarlet thread that binds the epochs, each
To each; one chain, the links indissoluble,
Which binds the earth to heaven and the universe;
One hand, discerned by only those who'll see,
That ever points unwavering to—The Cross,
As every new development in six
Creative days, prepare and render better
Fitted the earth for man, to whom they point.
This simplifies and gives a mighty grasp
Upon all truth whate'er is worth our pains
To learn or know; takes elevated points
Of view, and gives a range of vision vast,—

Far in extent as is the universe,—
The past and future,—all that was and is
And is to come for earth, and man and angel—
The finite most allies to infinite:
As from a mountain peak, exceeding great
And high, we see a landscape beautiful
And large, extending far, but seen in one
View, panoramic, lying at our feet.
To render truth complex, misty, confused
Requires but little brain, or none at all,
And error oftener indicates than truth.
To simplify and render few the truths
Revealed in life, the world and universe
Is the office of mind both of man and angel.

One theme by angel tongues was now discussed:—
Will God abandon to the powers of hell
This new created world, one empire more
Added to increase their strength where they may range
And rule, insulting His omnipotence?
Will He endure to have the fiends obscure
His glory, sole end and aim of all His works,—

And thus be thwarted by the powers of hell?
    His all-sufficiency is adequate
To meet whatever crisis may occur
In His vast realms, in earth or heaven or hell.
E'en warring fiends' wrath, from the abyss,
He makes to praise His Majesty, and more
Firmly to establish His eternal throne.
The end He seeth of all the universe
Of matter and intelligence, ere first
Beginning was to e'en a star in space.
Alone in the awful silence of the past
Eternity, appalling His abode,
He all nature contemplated synthetic
And co-existent. When He ordered time
Began to every world throughout the vast
Immensity, the arena where He works
Progressively, that creature minds may grow,
Expand, be glorified in apprehending
The mighty God, Creator of all things.

    The era which began with man created
Holy, dawned luminously upon the earth,

And was the first of this redemptive day.
His fall commenced to draw the evening shades
Around the world and mantled all in gloom,
Which darker grew until the era ends.

 Amid each era's darkest hour light breaks
Forth in meridian day—in noonday splendor,
By Power Supreme, advancing something new,
More perfect, looking to maturity,—
To issue ultimately in the glow
Of Heaven, when clouds shall all have passed away.
'Tis thus with every Christian life upon earth :
Day dawns when darkest clouds eclipse our path—
In hours of sorrow, pain or death—when all
Seems dark, the heart faint, sinking in despair !
Then oftenest power divine relief bestows.
They're wheels within a wheel, which illustrate,
Shed light upon, make clear a mighty truth !

 Adam and Eve reclining in the cool
Of day out in the open firmament,
Now heard Jehovah's voice, as from a dream
Awaked, and fearing hid among the Garden's

Foliage, hoping thus their guilt to hide.
Thus guilty conscience ever since has done-
In efforts to conceal reveals her guilt.
What wing so swift as to elude the eye
Of God and lurk unknown beyond the sky?
For all within the air or heaven abides,
Or even if beyond the bounds of space,
Are nigh and open to His piercing sight!
The voice called, and they came,—not blithe,
Joyful and gay as wont to meet their Lord,
But sad, reluctant and with faltering step,
And began to excuse their nakedness
In plea for hiding. Then their Lord inquired,
How they'd obtained this knowledge,—whether they'd
Transgressed and tasted the forbidden fruit?
Adam confessed his guilt—too evident;
A guilt which bore already fruit of shame,—
For coward he'd become—accused his wife—
The lovely Eve, heaven's gift,—for whom before
He'd suffer death: and she the serpent's guile.
Whereupon hearing this, the Lord pronounced
The serpent cursed above all beasts, because

The instrument of Satan's wiles, and added :
Between thee and the woman enmity
Exists henceforth, and between thine and her seed :
It thy head shall bruise, thou shalt bruise his heel.
    Thus was announced a prophecy, the germ
And sum developed since in history :
So is the oak entire in the acorn hid.
God's purpose to redeem the world was thus
And now revealed—the first display of grace
The universe had known—the advance of force
And penalty which devils had endured,
And will endure eternally, so far
As known. Without renouncing royalty
Divine, nor silencing the thunder peals
Of wrath 'gainst sin, revealed in law enforced—
Exhibited in might and fittingly
Upon Sinai when to Israel law was given—
God's voice in love and mercy spake in words
Of cheer, and lighted all the gloom of Eden,
And echoed sweetly in man's heart depraved.
In meekness suffering wrong, while love illumes
The countenance, and with forgiving grace

Beams sweetly upon the hands which cruelly
Afflict, malignant spirits least endure,
Whether they're wicked men or ugly devils.
The letter kills, but spirit giveth life—
A maxim having application far
And wide, not simply to the spiritual,—
But natural, for sweetest earthly life
Is love unfeigned in all its purity :—
The law enforced destroys, but love redeems.
This to the human pair was cheering news,
Like the anchor to mariners tempest-tossed
Nearing rocks and shoals, and grim death at hand.
    This still small voice of love Elijah heard
When hunted by the wicked Jezebel.
In Horeb's deep recesses hidden, neither
A blast of wind that rent and brake the rocks,
Nor an earthquake that rocked the mount as waves
A vessel in a storm, nor liquid fire
That glowed and ran in streams throughout the mount
Moved him. But when the voice of God was heard,
With mantle wrapped about his face, he went
And reverent stood to learn and heed heaven's message.

Oh, sweet still voice! Here is Jehovah's mild
And radiant presence felt more than His power
Or wisdom or benevolence. 'Tis love
Revealed to guilty man, a voice that grew
In accents clear and more distinct since first
Both Adam and Eve heard the promise given
Until Immanuel came, the Second Adam,
To restore our fallen and rebellious race.

    When 'gainst the serpent was pronounced the curse,
The Lord turned to the human pair. First Eve,
Because the first in sin, and through the mother
Her daughters since were sentenced to endure
Great pains in childbearing, and her desire
Subject to the husband's, who should o'er her rule.
The ruling savors of our fallen state:
The more a husband rules, makes manifest
Authority over his loving wife,
The more he proves himself an imbecile,
Or Satan's kin, allied to him in fact,
Applying to his kind the curse imposed
Too readily, who ought himself be ruled!
For Adam's sake the ground was cursed: with toil,

Sorrow and in pain bread should be produced.
Though so symmetrical in beauty, death's
Warrant was added,—doomed like noxious beasts
His body must die and return to dust.
Anticipating death, which none can know
But once, how terrible must it have seemed,
Which daily met his eye on every side ;
And fear must have possessed his soul! The life
However of the soul could ne'er become
Extinct, though all the chilling waves of sin
From hell should roll their hideous billows o'er it.
Hence doubtless Enoch from the pains of death
Was saved, because in purity of heart
He walked with God : occurring in this era,
Which does not terminate until the flood.

    The Judge and Saviour of mankind thus brought
His present mission to a close, and quick
As thought the farthest stars were reached, His time
Of flight unmeasured, distance great or small
Alike to Him, for infinite Himself,—
And only known when He Himself reveals

To heaven or earth or hell, or man or angel—
Without a body limited to space,
As yet, of either flesh or spirit form,—
Except assumed for temporary use,
A form in semblance like to man or angel,—
From elements, which the Almighty power
Can fashion into any image willed.
Hence often He appeared in human form,
And just as quickly vanished as thin air.
Not marvellous if Spirit Power who gave
The elements their Being and who forms
Them into everything we see and know,
Should take therefrom and fashion any form
In which to act and compass His designs.

To angels now 'twas known that man was saved.
To earth with one accord they turned their gaze.
In Paradise the human pair there still
They saw, and breathless admiration, love
And wonder stilled each throbbing heart, and heaven
Was still as when man's sad fall was announced.
No sound save streams pellucid rolling through

.The ivory palaces in murmurings sweet
Was heard : such silence brought from sudden joy,
And inexpressible, hearts cannot long
Endure in quietude.   Their gushing souls
O'erflowing with love soon found vent in tears.
Unlike before when man fell, they now wept
For very joy—as angels weep—a joy
Such as alone heaven feels, all peaceful, mild,
Serene.   Oh ! the consummate joy of Heaven !
Comparatively we are ignorant
As yet of the redeemed and Holy City,
Though prophets wrote inspired.   Nor Seraph's tongue
Can Heaven portray to man :—a language spoken
There unintelligible below the skies.
Oh, Holy City, everlasting realms
Of bliss, our paradise of love restored,
Beautified, how thy glorious beams enwrap
Our minds when nearing thy celestial heights ;
When zephyrs odoriferous fan our brow
Sweating from weary toil ; when songs are heard
Produced by angels joining saints in praise !
There our beloved departed, thrilled with joy,

Shall our first entrance see and rush to meet
Our fond embrace—our coming long delayed
To eager eyes upon heaven's battlements!

 How wonderful is power Omnipotent
In matter first revealed—the elements,
The frame and body of the earth and stars;
In life, succeeding next, of trees and plants
And flowers—which moulds and beautifies the first,
To utilize and to adorn the earth;
In spirit, next succeeding, which discerns
Itself, enjoys its life and acts at will;
In conscience next, engraft in spirit life,
Which ministers supreme a heavenly bliss;
In sin,—which dares the conscience to inflict
Its penalties and violates its laws,
The laws of spirit when advanced to know
The right from wrong, and independent acts.
The conscience when inviolate is day,
And sinned against is night in spirit worlds!
Redemption next, the power and grace of God—
Power infinite, grace marvellous and new,

Of Heaven's King to save a creature in
His image made, from spirit shades and death;
Then glory follows next and last, as day
The rising sun, the seventh wonder in
The galaxy, both grand and luminous,
For time, eternity, the world and Heaven!

   To learn this new thing in the universe
Of wonders, how God though just can redeem
A creature fallen, now hence employs the minds
Angelic, from the bud of promise given
Until mature: upon each development
They sweetly talk together face to face
By twos or companies in heaven's vast plains,
A mighty host, and wonder and adore.
How conscience waked, illumed both here and more
Hereafter by heaven's light and purity,
Can cease to torture is a mystery—
Sleeping for future ages to reveal!
'Tis easier to understand how God
Forgives and saves, than that the soul can cease
To chide, afflict and torture its own self

For violence against itself in sin!
The conscience knows no mercy; hears no voice
Of grief; is like the adder closing the ear
Against the charmers charming ne'er so wisely.
Heaven fain would heed the prayer which conscience
    spurns.
Thus light is shed upon the affecting scene
Of Jesus weeping o'er Jerusalem—
Heaven weeping o'er the nature that repels
Its proffered love and touching sympathy!

    A further work remained. Man could not long
In Eden nigh the tree of life remain:
For now the interdicted tree; its fruit
For holiness and life was forfeited.
Death follows sin by nature's laws and will
Divine. Man's readiness his Maker's voice
To disobey foreseen. Now lest he also
Take of the tree of life and eat and live
Forever—vile, corrupt, depraved and foul,
Body and soul—God in love intervened.
    From all intelligences, cherubim

And seraphim, and angels both of death
And life, and from a host innumerable
God chose His ministers; to each a work
Assigned. Their mission known, equipped with power
Derived, they with their King descended straight
To earth, an armament imposing, grand
And irresistible. The Lord then drave
The man from Paradise, and at the east
Of Eden in the garden placed the dire
Cherubim with a flaming sword, which all
Approach cut off and guarded every way
Direct or winding to the tree of life.
Thus Adam was denied the taste or touch
Of what was once his food ambrosial—such
As heaven ministers to spirit life.

    The angels clothed with terror's ghastly robe,
And having in their hands the arrows barbed
With death, their stand resumed upon the earth.
These angels evil have power over man
To torment him with storms and chilling winds,
Producing sickness, pain and dire distress.

Thus Satan was given power over Job
To sweep away his princely wealth and leave
Him poor as when he came into the world,
To afflict and destroy his family,
And render sick and sore and vile his flesh.
Thus chastened often are we for rest when storms
Are o'er and shadows shall have fled away.
Thus evil angels, alway unconsciously,
Are heaven's messengers for final good.
Afflictions thus are blessings in disguise.
The soul sustained by Hand imperial
Reposes childlike in the arms divine,
Which ever round His sons beloved are thrown,
Though sore emotions struggle in the breast.

    The angels with sweet cordial from the fount
Of life then too assumed their ministry:
O'erburdened hearts allaying with the oil
Of gladness; carrying the stream of life
Unbroken, clearer, brighter through the wreck
Of our fallen race with types and prophecies—
Though not then fully understood—and giving
Hope, cheer and gladness; oft a human form

Assuming radiant in their holiness,
To speak with man and utter words of peace
And comfort, and the future joy reveal.
With tender wakefulness they bend their gaze,
Their wings outstretched, upon the earth and man,
Hovering always near, solicitous
For those committed to their sacred trust.
Undazzled by the scenery of heaven,
Its grandeur, beauty or its wealth, they cast
Benignant, loving looks upon the sons
And daughters of the earth to bless and save.

   From Paradise the human pair were driven
In order to effect a good :—to save
The pure from harlotry with the impure,
The good from coalescing with the evil.
Heaven for hell has no affinity :
Yet hell's design and effort is to get
Within the gates of heaven and subdue
The good and pure to her foul purposes.
'Tis hell's most artful and successful mode
Of warfare 'gainst what's good in earth and heaven.

When done the knell to peace and happiness
Is tolled, as when the serpent entered Eden.

    Disaster comes and never fails to come
When Satan makes inroads into the church:
The church becoming then so dangerous
And foul and cruel as to shock the world.
Nor does a shock e'er fail in such a case
Less than earthquake fires warring fiercely 'neath
The surface of our globe to toss and rend
A continent and trouble isles and seas.
A vessel rides securely every sea,—
Until the waters get within—then sinks
O'erpowered by that which erst she tossed aside,
Or proudly used to reach a distant haven.
'Tis Satan's pleasing argument which fools
And knaves employ, too often in God's name,—
The world must be impressed and won, and sin
Subdued and sinners saved by coalescing
Therewith in some degree, conformity
A trifle, innocent to patronize,
Propitiate and take the world by guile!

The church, thus duped and self-deceived, is like
A silly toad that gives itself away
And hops into a hungry serpent's maw.
A church, God's children using subtlety,
Unskilled in handling weapons of the pit,
Deserve and surely come to woful grief!
In modern times church fairs and festivals
And concerts, feasts and lotteries devised
'Tis said to run the church—*but to the Devil!*
A sin substantially which brought the flood
And every overthrow the world has seen.
But 'tis the sure road to prosperity—
Short-lived, but this is seen, alas! too late;
To wealth and rich adornments such as please
The world—and Satan too: he helps the church
More than his devotees allied to him
In faith and works belonging to the world—
In evil faith and works are ne'er divorced,
When pious frauds, concerts, theatricals
Are introduced in houses consecrated—
O mockery! to God for prayer and praise;
And hinders not the battle, only seeming

Against his kingdom, and the while deludes.
'Tis then like Samson in Delilah's lap,
Shorn of its strength while dandled into dreams :—
Then Satan laughs and hell is all aglee :
For churches spirit power possess for good
In naught but what is holy, right and true.

    The Upper Room, but poor and lone and drear
'Mid Salem's palaces of wealth and towers
Of strength, where sorrowing disciples prayed
In solitude, is to the church a Fount
Of blessing, a well-spring of light to each
Succeeding age, to teach how best—nay ! how
Alone to reach the heights of heavenly bliss,
The source of every good—unfailing power,
And bring a blessing down to barren earth !
The earth still feels the power which emanates
Therefrom, still cherishes the gifts bestowed
Upon that most eventful night the world
Has seen or felt, still hears as every age
Has heard the tongues which there became inspired.
Oh, Mighty Spirit, Presence Infinite,
All Heaven is illumed and brightly glows

With Thy most tranquil beauty, grace and love,
Oh! come to earth again, to praying saints
As in the Upper Room, renowned, and show
From heaven's ethereal shores Thy wealth of love;
Make guilty earth to tremble with Thy blasts,
And with Thy tempest power brake stony hearts!
O Spirit! hover o'er us—dead to Thee,
And suddenly brake cloven tongues of flame
Upon our heads—a light from Heaven to earth—
A flame from holy altars given to man,
And quicken us into a life and power
Akin to Thine—the only power that saves,
Either the church, the world, or human souls!
Oh, tender Spirit! live and breathe within
The church; oh, loving Presence, sweet beyond
Our thought, abide with us, and let us see
Thy glance of love and Heaven in that glance!
    The Upper Room reveals a church in shade
Or light, with spirit power for ill or good!

    After man's fall the righteous coalesced
With the wicked, dissolute and carnal,—looked

Upon the daughters of the world and took
Them wives of all the fair and beautiful:
The sons of Seth with daughters fair of Cain!
Dark clouds conceal from view this period,
And little can we penetrate behind
The scenes. But this much clearly we discern
From Scripture, that the church in harlotry
With man and devils, fused the good and evil,—
Became thus secularized and corrupt.
The good amalgamated with the bad.
Hence lust soon soiled, befouled and sank the
    church
In sin which God not long could tolerate,
Inducing Him to bring the flood upon
The earth : which ends this era of the world's
History on the first redemptive day.
In gloom and night and death each era ends
Because the church joins sacrilegiously
And is at one with schemes and wickedness
Resorted to and practised by the world!
No sin more grieves the loving heart of God
And surely brings disaster, pain and death.

While Noah safely sailed the one vast sea
Above the deluged world and sleeping dead,
Alone saved with his family, then dawned
The second era of man's history.
The righteous preacher, faithful, true, devout,
Who for more than a century withstood
The taunts of dissolute and wicked men;
Undaunted by their threats; unmoved by jeers;
And undiscouraged labored on, though all
A deaf ear to his faithful message gave,
Was reaping now his rich well-earned reward.

Not less a lesson here than a rebuke
Is given to all who estimate the worth,
Capacity and fitness for the task
Of preaching by the measure of success,
So called, to be reported and extolled—
But piously in tone befitting saints,
Each year in presbytery and in print.
David's great sin of numbering the people,
Through pride, and suffering in consequence

A plague, some pastors reckless, false to trust,
Forget,—or else expound to suit the times.
'Tis called, Reports upon religious state
Of churches.* The intent is doubtless good,

---

* WITHHELD STATISTICS.—How it would startle some of our congregations to have the pastor follow the reading of the annual report of his church with a few of the withheld statistics, somewhat after this sort :— "Of the thirty-two who have joined our church the past year I find that five of those who came in on profession have unmistakably fallen into former evil ways, while of those who were received by letter three were certainly lacking in good character in the churches they left, although by the record they were in 'good and regular standing.' One of our elders is popularly reported to have swindled a neighbor outrageously in a notorious business transaction. We have lost one of our more prominent members by his transfer to the county jail on conviction of crime. A careful examination of our record has convinced me that fully one-third of our members can be counted on the 'dead-head' list. They do nothing in the line of Christian activity. As to their example, they are not bad enough to be a warning to the outside world, nor good enough to be taken as an example by anybody—in or out. Our benevolent contributions look pretty well for our numbers, but I learn that nearly one-third of their full amount has been given by four persons; and that of the other members of the church more than one-half gave less to religious causes than they pay toward public amusements, while there are not a few families which gave more for peanuts during the year than they put in the contribution box. A fair estimate of the tobacco bills of the congregation is twice and three-eighths the amount given by the church to home and foreign missions combined." Such a supplement as this, in kind and in degree according to the particular community, could be truthfully made in many a church where the annual report last presented is spoken of as "every way encouraging."—*Sunday-School Times.*

But many, snared thereby, report themselves,
Relate too often only partial facts,
Adroitly hide whate'er is damaging,
And brethren praise who'll in return praise them—
A mutual admiration feast, in love
Each one with self, absorbed in greed of praise ;
A vanity fair—bart'ring each the others—
And silly they fail to discern when sold,
For spirit power just then is stupefied
By glittering bombast and flattery.
While scepticism abounds and churches die,
And piety is low and at discount
Is this for puerile compliments the time,—
Not less obsequious than footmen serve ?
Itching ears listen while proud hearts relate
The numbers added to their church, converted
The pastors say, for which they're truly thankful—
To build themselves upon the work they've done !
They err who judge the Lord by feeble saints !
And much, alas ! the issue proves is only
Man's work : but what's the odds ? Conventions hear,
Applaud, assign to fat and wealthy fields

The boasters lusting for the loaves and fishes.
Hypocrisy! that's robed in pious terms!
The bravest, best and faithful witnesses
Who're either modest or unfortunately
Too good and conscientious to conform
To tendencies that both corrupt the church
And shame its true ambassadors, are either
Silenced or given places poor and lone—
Good for the churches served, but bad for them!
They're failures in ecclesiastical
Politics, have demurred upon artifice:
They've not exalted self, nor sought for place
In lines of sure promotion, seeking fame,
And wealth and ease and elegance, and none
Will do it for them,—nor discern their worth!
By them a pyrotechnical display
Has not been given—in religious news,
Weekly; nor have they editors cajoled
To keep their names with puffs before the churches.
Hence forest parishes, or any place
Is deemed by brethren (!) good enough for them :—
And then the while each one is estimated

By places occupied—gauged by their wealth :
No matter how obtained—'tis immaterial,
And none would venture rashly to inquire—
Of course 'tis Providence, whose guidance each
Has sought, 'tis said, to indicate their duty.
Hypocrisy will hide her face for once
And blush, and know and feel herself outdone !
Hence many a pure and faithful minister
Unknown, uncared for, soon forgotten dies
In poverty, of whom the world's unworthy :—
Their cries and moans voiced by the plaintive winds ;
And solitudes and glens and caves alone
In sympathy give ear and weep responsive !

    They're blessèd, passive, patient poor, who're loved,
Of Heaven, despised of earth,—whose secret lives
Are deep and understood by few,—who stoop
Beneath the cares of life with fettered feet
And listless, wrapped in deep, but silent thought ;
And homeless, shuffled here and there, alone
Within a world which has no love for them,
No sympathy—and deemed but in the way :—
Perhaps the meek and chastened smile that comes

And goes, is God within the friendless soul ;—
Perhaps the light which now and then illumes
Their brow, and shines from wan and wasted cheeks
Is from the angels hovering both near
And o'er their heads, which baffle mortal sight,
But waiting, wings outspread, to waft their charge
To blissful realms when death appears and severs
Gently their spirit from the earth and clay !
The soul by sorrow's chastening touch becomes
Too pure for earth to know or see or love ;
So lovely shines, so sweetly beams, that earth
And sin their face avert and turn aside !·
Perhaps! alone in barren Patmos isle, ·
Exiled in place and state, there's vision given
As glorious as but once beheld,—hence sight
Becomes impaired to earthly things and dim,
While spirit is absorbed by bliss revealed,—
Which earth esteems defects, and riots o'er,
And quickly shuffles them to solitudes
And barrenness, as was the Apostle John !

  Such prophets, learned in theologic lore,—
Such Christians, mellowed meek in love with **God**,—

Such servants, freighted with experience,—
The church too often deems superannuated :
And lusts and lisps for sophomoric lore,—
For brazen declamation, loud in cry
And boisterous as infantile in thought,—
For lightly freighted crafts to sail smooth seas—
From parent's tutelage removed too soon,
Which wreck themselves and crew ere port is reached !
    Soul ne'er becomes impaired by age, and ne'er
Loses what's once been learned, nor ever less
Of power or force exerts when circumstanced
To act in normal strength, though brain may palsy,
Become impaired and feeble like the body.
The spirit form assumed in blissful realms,
Rejuvenated, it will act with more
Than wonted strength, and have an instrument
Through which to act which never will impair.
The young divines who're humble and sincere,
Without ambition to exalt themselves,
Who pray to serve the poor and sorrowing,
Who're learned and well equipped to serve the church,
Are heaven's best gift, a legacy of love

To earth and churches seeking help from God,—
Noble men, reaping precious fruit for Heaven—
Who'll nobler be when bending 'neath the weight
Of years of toil while grace illumes their brow.

   Severe denunciations hurled against
Any who serve at sacred altars, holy,
Howe'er just, modern thinkers deem unkind,—
Unfriendly to the church our Saviour bought.
But what if they're against the evils, rank
And sore, which left unchecked would soon destroy
The church and world, blood bought by love divine?
The surgeon's knife will sever quivering limbs
Diseased, regardless of the patient's cries
And tears, and yet in love his task perform!
The church can ne'er with safety to the world,
Herself or men in witness-bearing fail,
In equity and truth come short in service,
Through fear or policy ignore a wrong,
And hence herself must be and keep most pure;
As salt kept savory and light unquenched;
Be vigilant and more concerned to quench

Evils which are within than those without.
Hereby are known Earth's righteous noblemen.
'Tis hatred of impurity that hurls
And renders true the darts to pierce the shields.
Whate'er is human may become impure,
Or err or fail in duty that's imposed.
Darts damage not through human agency
The spirit pure, what's holy or divine.
The church which God has saved, protects and loves
Is not a bauble gilded for the eye
Of sense and glittering in borrowed light,
A toy of every wanton breeze in air
And ready momentarily by touch
Or rank breath to collapse and disappear!
The world detracts where saints conceal a guilt.
But honesty in churches strength imparts,
Though many for fidelity endure
And suffer patiently for years in quiet.
If we would judge ourselves, we'd not be judged.
But all can see where much applies, applaud
And guilt adjudge to others, not to self.
Alas! there's guilt attached to not a few .

Where churches wane and guilt supinely yawns
With folded hands and groans and ask the cause !
    The question paramount is, whether good
Or evil dominates. 'Tis not against
The good and pure and holy in the church
To hear that many learned and noble men,
Servants of God, are in obscurity
Suffering from neglect and wrong of which
The church is chargeable and piety
Is made to blush ! Should Truth with visage bright
Sublimely stand with eyes of fire and speak
In plainness, multitudes in places rich
And well intrenched would howl against the rash
Intruder 'pon their realm of elegance—
Bereft of Spirit Power and shorn of strength—
And count him sore ; one who has failed to please—
A worldly church and young effeminates ;
One who has enemies—a sycophant
Would be preferred by such who're worldly wise ;
A churlish fellow—published such as by
A dunghill feathered tribe, because forsooth
He treads too near a setting hen, alarms

Her henship and awakes her cackling ire,—
In which the harem join and sympathize.
  The temper of our speech is moderate.
Zion, her daughters, sons and citizens
Should lovingly protect, adorn and bless,
And spread a halo glory round the earth,
Encompassing and filling every place
And heart—than Saturn's rings more beauteous.
Unseemly hence for her to maledict,
Or taunt or curse when evils are exposed
That tarnish, dim or hide her glory fair ;
Detract or anger, goad or persecute
When called upon to heal her blemishes—
But thus unwittingly proclaims abroad,
Aloud, then evident if not before,
Her conscious guilt and shame, through pride concealed !
Her face so beautiful in purity
Henceforth and then becomes repulsive, dark
And low'ring, ugly, wrathful, dangerous,—
Like maidens fair defloured by hateful ire.
'Tis Zion's loving office tenderly
To soothe and heal a burdened, broken heart ;

To lift the fallen, cheer the faint and help
Our sinful race to realms of bliss and Heaven.
A church and clergy arrogant are base.
A fellow pilgrim, with averted face
To pass disdainfully and mock his cries,
Is spirit finite power in exercise
For ill and hateful to the good and pure,—
Is spirit fiendish and not of Zion !
To plead the cause and battle for the poor
And sorrowing in need is Zion's office,
Whereby spirit power best promotes earth's glory.

'Tis feared and felt that Agencies are too
Solicitous to credit with success
Their schemes, sustain fat salaries and chairs,
And build themselves upon their enterprises.
We've advertised a dearth of ministers,—
While multitudes are unemployed, prepared
And willing, nay ! solicitous for work ;
And seminaries to theology
Sacred, with others like employed compete—
Unseemly and unchurchly is the strife,

Each for itself alluring aspirants
For ministerial robes within their walls,
By scholarships and money to entice
Proportioned by the wealth that each controls;
And men renowned and usefully employed
In other less inviting fields, are called
To chairs regardless of the hurt inflicted,—
For called, the voice—of God, 'tis said—of self
Aggrandizement, 'tis feared—determines choice
Too often not less in church than in the State;—
Who may the proper sentiments possess,
In charity to their intelligence
We'll urge, but simply their expression hide,
Repress, as sorrow's hid at times by some
When keenly, pungently 'tis felt and weeps
Within, behind the scenes in solitude:
Some will presume to think, sometimes aloud,—
And for themselves without the aid of others.
We're told 'tis all to glorify the church.
Alas! the glory of the Agencies
Are neither modestly concealed nor named!
Their spirit power is thus concealed or lost.

And Colleges too founded for the church
By righteous men of old, in prayer and tears,
A worthy ministry to educate,—
Not little puerile vanity display
In graduating sons with great éclat,
With sound of cornet, flute and psaltery,
And sackbut, harp and dulcimer,—inviting
All to adore the Image that's set up !—
And cringe and fawn beneath the feet of wealth,
And kiss the hands whence rich endowments come !
Too often sceptics, who're called scientists,
Are given chairs, and clergymen who're good
And wise refused, when to the church they owe
Life and prosperity—waxed gross by wealth,
In foreign arrogance—to Satan sold !—
And innocently inquire,—why now so few
The ministry, the sacred office enter ?
Their understanding or the sacred word
If they'd consult, and turn aside one brief
Moment from vain imaginings, they'd know
The truth and render service to the world.
A wonder justly ought to be expressed

If any should religiously inclined
Become, and enter e'en the sacred church
In fellowship with saints from Satan saved!
  In culture intellectual history *
Records no ministry the world has seen
So learnéd, eloquent and strong for great
Achievements.   Danger lurks in pride of heart.
The baser metals burnishing will ne'er
Transform to precious : culture exercised
With zeal will only help, can ne'er produce
A man of God, or render pure the heart.

---

* "It is the sure indication of a living Christianity that so many of its preachers are drawn from the most successful men in other walks of life. They could not be at peace or feel themselves to be obedient to the heavenly vision until they had accepted the sacred vow and ordination. An elect ministry like this, called to be apostles by the will of God and by the resistless yearnings of the Spirit of God within them, were never more needed than to-day, and all others were never more out of place. Of good men, and good lives, and good service the church and the world can never have too many. But there is nothing gained and much lost in thrusting men merely because they are good, or accepting them merely because they are willing, into this *high* calling of God. God wants something more than pegs to fill 'vacancies.' He demands projectiles, with His own Divine Forces behind them, mighty through God to the pulling down of strongholds."

Their learning rightly guided, humble, pure,
Beneath their strokes would Satan's kingdom totter
And doubtless fall.   Among them found are men
Who're great and good and pure in heart, who love
The church, and cheerfully would sacrifice
Their all and life itself to testify
Their faith, if 'twere required for the truth.
Hence tendencies which render insecure,
The weaknesses endangering the church
Most readily the church will rectify
When clearly by the wise and good exposed,
If purity therein predominates.
A bridge no stronger is than the weakest link
Which with the others holds its ponderous weight.
Where'er a danger is, fidelity,
Learning, experience or art detect,
Expose and deem both the security
Of structure and the lives of multitudes
Of greater moment, incomparable,
Than shielding men in charge from merited
Censure, displacement, or e'en sacrifice.
   Thus is the glory of the church by clouds

Often o'ercast, as evening follows morn,
As shade succeeds the light in every era,
Showing that perfect happiness the earth
Forbids to man, and perfect beauty too.
But greater light has always followed gloom,
And brighter eras from those more obscure,—
Developed from imperfect traits—for nought
Is perfect here, as clouds obscuring light
Collect and part to let the sun shine through—
Brighter than had the clouds not intervened.
Man's duty hence is clear,—to labor on
In faith and prayer and love, and ne'er forget
That Spirit Power is high enthroned above
The petty powers, unfriendly to the church,
Or ills which unawares do creep therein ;
That earth is moving to elysian fields,
And gloom or death is but transition state.
By battling for what's pure we best promote
Our strength—prepare the soul for higher life.
Happy the men who're foremost in the strife,
And recognize beneficence in ills
Which call in exercise their spirit power,—

Who scorn to cringe, prefer to die than yield
To wealth and arrogance, which adder like,
Possess the fang and poison too that kills!
   We need not only desolation see;
We need not wander walled in darkness round,—
And ne'er within and ne'er without see light,
As bondsmen boast their chains, and scoff at love
That fain would scatter clouds or set them free.
Who have the light should make it brighter glow;
And faith make greater—cultivate to sight,
To sweetest worship—into splendors hide;
In plainness chide where wrongs are known, but love—
The glow of Heaven, illuming every word!

   As Noah reaped a harvest long delayed,
So faithful labor ultimately brings
Reward in this—or in the world to come.
Many are true and faithful, mourning o'er
Evils they're powerless to eradicate,—
Nay! multitudes to duty as discerned,
According to the light possessed are true.
Pastors, in being too solicitous

About success or seeming failure, err.
With measured step and stooping low in grief
And sorrow, judgment Noah preached, without
Design or ill intent, and none would hear
Or turn to God and seek the peace of Heaven.
Yet he and family were blessed and saved.
Man e'en the judge and churches carnalized,
Fidelity is better than success.

    This era dawns as did the first with promise.
The beautiful rainbow arching the heavens
Over the sweet but lately deluged earth,
Of Heaven's covenant a fitting sign,
Which often Noah had admired before,
Was now of God designed and pointed out
The sign of promise for all future time,
That every generation following
When looking 'pon the bow within the clouds
Might realize that God is merciful,—
That it encircles too His great white throne!
    The era wanes when Noah's family
Had multiplied upon the plains as rich

As Eden on the river banks along
Euphrates, and were one in speech and aim.
The church again drawn in the strong whirlpool
Of lust and worldly schemes was nearly lost.
To recognize its visage fair 'twas hard,
Or to distinguish it amid the world
Of lust and vanity, in greed of power.
With one accord they reasoned to erect
A tower to defy the powers of heaven,
And render it a city of refuge
And defence, whose top should reach 'bove the
    clouds,—
A city of renown throughout the earth.
Confusion then of speech by Spirit Power,
To save the church and render her distinct
And known, the second era terminates:
That separate, a church and people, set
Apart for God, elected from the world,
For service might be kept, both true and holy.
Contamination with the world, the church
In league with Satan, God ne'er long endures.
For wrath begins and soon, and judgment too,

When God's elect have oneness with the world.
Nations and men into the lowest hells
Of vile iniquity may sink and sport
Themselves, and God forbear to punish long,
For even generations let continue
And suffer them to prosper in the world:
But when the church defiles herself, becomes
With sin most foul, then judgment is at hand.

    The era third with Abraham begins,
A patriarchal age in history,
And ends with Israel's sad captivity
In Egypt's garden of delights along
The Nile. The promise of deliverance,
Vouchsafed of heaven, more clearly now appears:—
In him should all the families of earth
Be blessed. His promised seed should multiply,
Subdue, redeem and save the earth from sin's
Sad blight by means of one, a Saviour yet
To come. With faith he heard the gospel news
In glad delight, and henceforth was the friend
Of God, accredited and true, the son

Of heaven and righteous in the sight of angels.
His piety and faith were prominent,
Guilty of but few lapses, honestly
Recorded, showing his mortality;
Refusing to ally his son and heir,
Isaac, with the polluted Canaanites;
Who talked familiarly as friend to friend
With God in human form,—persistently
Used forceful speech to turn Him from His purpose
To destroy wicked Sodom and Gomorrah;
Who reverenced Melchisedek, because
A priest and consecrated to the Lord.
A mighty prince; renowned and valiant; strong
Enough to conquer kings, and generously
Refusing to take any part of spoil;
Of courteous, modest, meek and dignified
Demeanor, truly one of royal blood.
In generosity few men before
Or since his time have equalled Abraham.
Though having prior right because of age,
Kinship and wealth to choose himself the place,
And fattest of the land in which to dwell

And feed vast multitudes of flocks and herds
Which had accumulated upon his hands,
He generously suffered Lot to choose
While from a mountain peak, exceeding high,
Together they viewed and discussed the whole
Of Palestine. The valley lying low,
Guarded by mountains, through which Jordan flows
And renders rich and fragrant all the plane,
Lot coveted for its wealth, and remarked
Upon its being rich and beautiful
As Eden in its wealth of luxury
Original. Hence there he went with all
His flocks, dependents, families and wealth,
And dwelt with wicked Sodomites, a prince
Himself, and so esteemed throughout the plane.
But Abraham was still content to dwell
In tents at Hebron, 'mong the sterile hills,
For prayer and meditation, hid almost
From the world's view in close obscurity,
And loved his quiet peaceful home above
Beersheba or all of Palestine.
    Thus Lot was snared and suffered poverty

And final overthrow in punishment
For covetousness, while Abraham grew
Stronger, increased in wealth and in esteem
Of all the land in which he dwelt a prince.

    A prophecy the church has never learned,
And warning ever since unheeded, are
Here taught—unwelcome truth, but salutary.
The church too often, like Lot, has coveted
The world, its wealth and luxury ; has grown
Carnal in consequence ; is tottering
Upon the brink of ruin, then near its fall.
Unlike the Master when by Satan tempted
And offered all the kingdoms of the world,
Their wealth and glory, if He'd homage pay
To him, the prince and power of earth and air.
In England when the church was founded, cities
And valleys rich were chosen ; while the men
Of prayer, the Culdees, retirement sought,
Content with poverty, and preached the truth
With power and grace, and laid foundations strong
For all the future of the church of God,—

Safe while depending on Heaven's grace, divine,
And humbly laboring for the poor and lone,
And for the rich who've poverty of spirit,
Who're seeking God in deep humility.

   But modern times have sadly lapsed, look awry,
And tread with delicate feet the old paths.
There are within the church, 'tis said a few,
Divines who scheme and lust for wealth and power,
Applause and glitter of the world ; and seek,
Unseemly oftentimes, the fattest fields
Which seemingly offer to gratify
Unholy greed—ambition in the church !
   Their Master, owning all the spacious world,
Scarce room He found or sought to lay His head !
And O ! shall sinful man, bought by His blood,
On pleasure, self and greatness be intent ?
   Such patronizingly esteem the less
Favored—but call them, brethren,—tolerate
Their presence, oftentimes with seeming grace—
But courtly restiveness pronouncing them
The while intruders in their precious realms ;

Concerned for little in the church—except
'Twill minister to their luxuriant fields ;
Caring for few—except the prominent !

    Their Master's mission was to address the poor.
Alas ! that wealth and pleasure, speaking fair,
Should steal the heart from grace and love away !
So did the Jewish priests Barabbas choose
Instead of Christ the meek, poor Nazarene !
Not to the world and flesh quite dead enough,
Nor hid enough in spirit life with God !
Prosperity and wealth than poverty
And grief and pain 'tis harder much to bear.
We'll pity more than blame where fault is found !

    But teachers, prominent in schools, tell us :—*
The ministry is overstocked, such as
The clergy are ! True doubtless, boldly said,
And honest if they themselves photograph !

---

    * "Just now I am convinced," says one, " we are making too many doctors, such as they are ; too many lawyers, such as they are; too many ministers, such as they are." We judge from some articles which we have seen lately that some persons would be ready to extend the catalogue, and say "'too many professors, such as they are ; too many theological schools, such as they are."

Will they forgive if one who's meek and poor
And insignificant insinuates,—
The prominent may be the effervescence,
And likely are, because the most exposed
To tendencies defacing purity.
The violets, though modest, yet have worth
And beauty, fragrance—more esteemed and sought
Than sunflowers which stand stiffly eminent.*

Pastors who're shepherds of the flock, and such
In truth, and not accrediting themselves

---

* "There is no class of men for whom I have so much respect and affection as for average ministers of the Gospel," says Dr. Babb. "They are not sustained in their labors by popular applause and newspaper puffs, but by the love of Christ and the souls of men. They are patient, persevering, self-denying. They endure as seeing Him who is invisible. They lay the foundations for others to build upon. They do not estimate themselves at so many thousands a year, but are willing to work even though poorly paid and not highly esteemed of men, knowing that their reward is in Heaven. It is these average ministers who have extended the Church over this broad continent and established missionary stations around the world. Let us honor them as God does. Let us not provoke Him to anger by treating them with indifference or contempt. And if we ourselves are but average ministers in the estimation of the world, let us rejoice that God has counted us worthy; for to be His ambassador in some frontier settlement is nobler than to wear the crown of an emperor."

The wiser leaders of their silly sheep ;
Pastors who supervise the church of God,—
Not Sabbath clubs, composed of fash'nables,
Ignoring law and all authority,
Divine or human—license rampant in
God's house ; but pastors of the Master taught
Will shun, not seek, resorts of fashion, wealth
And pleasure, watering-places lewd with games,
Horse-racing, frolics which allure the world :
In virtues such not erudite and learned—
Defective education here will never
Virtue's fair face in light of day make blush.
There are who'll censure eloquently priests
Of Rome for hawking, fox-hunts and the like
In feudal times, long since, and deem them base
Because they catered to the sports of nobles,—
Compared, the modern more effeminate,
In which with zest and pleasure they'll engage,
Or else by mingling with the multitudes
Without protest give countenance thereto,
And in extenuation of their guilt
Claim need of rest—vacation ! is the term,

From active duties of the ministry—
Vacate themselves the while of Spirit Power !
The rest, forsooth, which fashionables enjoy
Is mockery to common sense, and more
Than mockery to need of rest alleged,
And to intelligence, of which the world's
Not quite bereft, but specious terms their true
Meaning, intent and force discerns, though silent.
'Twas doubtless pleasant with the Sodomites
Upon the banks of Jordan beautiful,
And dull and dreary 'mong the sterile hills
Of Hebron, yet the safer place for men
Of prayer to gather strength and rest the brain,
Without intoxicants which enervate
Body and mind, and quench all unction in
The heart. Our churches languish—reason why !
Let many seek the cause within themselves.
Indeed not long nor far we'll need to search !
The world perceives—is silent, or assents
With pleasure ill concealed, and winks and leers
If clergy do but dance the dance of death !
    Some people will indulge the damaging

Conceit, that ministers may make mistakes,
That clergymen may wrong themselves, their cause
Betray, or indirectly shame their trust !
    Divines who're eloquent to crimson pews,
If like their Master, angel eloquence
Would reach, enjoy a wholesome rest, gain much
In spirit power and vigor physical
By searching mountain glens and barren haunts
To help the poor and lone and sorrowing—
Who're perishing for lack of food, the bread
Of life ; and churches found for prayer and praise—
Where hitherto the air but voiced a curse ·
Or wail ; and bless eternally the homes
Which ne'er before have seen the light of Heaven !
  · 'Tis loss to places needing help and home
And clergymen themselves, to delegate
The work to brethren, poor in speech and purse—
But well would serve the churches founded by
The strong, while being nurtured into strength
By noble pastors of more wealthy fields.
Pastors too delicate and nice to serve
The Master thus, to touch with hands ungloved

The hardy poor—prefer a foreign tour,
Or dandling luxury upon the lap
Of wealth and fashion, ease and elegance,—
Are too remiss and lewd to serve at all!
The pastors who subdue the hearts of others
Must o'er themselves gain noble victory.

    Torpidity nor cowardice e'er helps
But enervates, especially in Zion
Which ought to know the truth and rectify
A wrong, and crushes hope in human hearts.
Alas! that aristocracy should yawn
And snore, or ever dominate in Zion,
Greatly imperilling her high intent
To feed the hungry, cheer the faint and help
The poor against a world's enslaving power!

    Jesus! Thy blessèd feet did hallow hill
And dale, and stony paths—all earth too Thine;
Were swift to run in quest of need, and didst
Disdain to tread the halls of kingly courts!
To poor outcasts, to wretched souls—despised
Of men, how amiable Thou wert, to cheer
And help and lift them from their fallen state!—

Didst feed the hungry with miraculous
Food, bread from heaven; and heal the sick, and soothe
The sorrowing, and raise the dead to life!
Disciples' feet by Thee were washed, though Lord
Of all the earth, to teach humility.
If self-abased we'll never fear a fall!
O! that like-minded we might be, to bless
Our race, not envy man's estate, but crown
Our life and death with blessings of the poor!
Then we'd upon the holy mountain feed,
Where Christ and His, in loving converse are,
Around eternal fountains and the streams
Of Paradise, transfigured each, and shine
As Jesus shone on Tabor's heights, sublime!
He wept o'er Salem's gross impiety
And consequent fall drawing near—the groans
And tears and blood and total overthrow
Which He foresaw; and at the grave with friends
In sympathy! O lovely Jesus, grant
Our spirit grace and beauty such as Thine,—
To serve our race as Thou hast done—from love—
As though no crown awaits our journey's end!

Man Redeemed.

Thus service in its light and shade appears.
Let each discern that lives are most o'ercast
Which glitter seemingly—in borrowed light!

The day grows brighter upon each era's dawn.
The fourth begins with Moses, signally
Prepared by Providence for his great work,
And ends with Saul made king, which terminated
The theocratic government that God
Ordained and regulated for man's best
Interests. Ne'er had there been prosperity
And safety better guaranteed since man
Had lost his purity. God's personal
Presence in might and love assured the good
Of every blessing human nature needs.
In Israel's long captivity in Egypt
The patriarchal prophecy seemed null
And void: The sceptre ne'er from Judah shall
Depart, nor a lawgiver from between
His feet, till Shiloh come. But Spirit Power
Reigned in the fiery furnace which tried Israel,
His chosen seed, the church upon the earth,

As in the burning bush which Moses saw,
Near Horeb unconsumed, or even singed.
The present era partially fulfils
The prophecy: for Moses qualified
And trained of Providence with marvellous
Care in the valley of the Nile, excelled
In learning by none other ancient land,
And in the Midian desert undistracted
By aught without with Jethro for his priest,
Became lawgiver to the church and world.
Also himself a prophet and a type
Became of Shiloh, the Messiah, yet
To come; and gave the church and was himself
The promise of deliverance from sin,
Which more enslaves than Egypt's despotism.

    The beauteous redemptive day drew nigh
When Moses, lovely babe, was claimed a prince
By one of Pharaoh's line of princesses.
Raised delicately, loved for personal
Beauty, admired by all he grew to man's
Estate with courtly manners, and possessed
Of all the learning Egypt had,—but chose

To suffer with the people whom God loved,
Rather than for a season to enjoy
The pleasures sin affords its votaries.
Wise, nevertheless a marvellous choice
For one with cultured gifts, pre-eminent,
And nigh the throne : aside from power divine
To prompt and guide and lovingly impel
The choice, he ne'er could have released himself
From sin's maelstrom, engulfing multitudes !

    God's presence personal, His agency
Immediate or mediate in all
Pertaining to His people, is the one
Great leading truth that underlies this era.
Hence came disaster, and the era waned
Into the shades of night and gloom intense
When Israel lusted for a king like other
Nations ; despised their birthright like Esau,
Who ne'er recovered it, though sought for long
And diligently with tears ; lost the favor
Of heaven, and were given a king in Saul
To satisfy and judge unholy lust
And their contemning heaven's gracious reign.

That they should recognize the agency
Of heaven, from bondage their release was wrought
By power alone divine; their passage through
The Red Sea on dry ground miraculous;
A cloud their guide and shield from heat by day;
A fiery pillar, luminous with heaven's
Splendor, to light them during tedious nights
And ever reassure a drooping faith.
The presence personal of God addressed
Their sight and hearing,—since their time no less
True than then, but addressing now our faith
And intellect: the presence then discerned
In clouds and fire and smoke,—in Sinai's mount
Which thundered words of terror in their ears,—
In Spirit Power which brake the flinty rock
And gave them drink, and gave them angels' food:
A presence all the same in modern times,
But differently revealed in consciences
And hearts of men, in love, the Holy Ghost
The agent, working upon and in man's spirit.
'Twas often then in wrath that God appeared,
The age of law given and enforced that kills,

, Condemns the sinner ; now the age of love,
Law having been enforced upon the Cross !

    How little understood, e'en in the church
Alas ! is God, divine and infinite.
Through spirit finite beauty is discerned
In earth and taste in food and smell in flowers
And brilliancy in stars and beauty known,
Enjoyed and loved in nature everywhere.
Without it all is dead to the universe,
And nothing is discerned or happiness
Affords,—for matter is inert and gross.
The blush upon the maiden's cheek, the glance
Given by the eye, the smile that sweetly comes
And goes, the words which fall from honeyed tongues
Are solely spirit giving through the flesh
Expression of itself.   The instrument
Of the soul, or spirit finite is the body.
But oh ! the difference between created
Spirits,—a chasm nearly infinite
Dividing each from others near akin.
Gorillas in the wilds of Africa

Have throats and tongues and voice, but only whine
And howl; a scavenger too has the same,
But speaks a jargon kindred to his work:
Beside them place a Jenny Lind, with organs
Of speech no different, but having great
Themes struggling in her soul and moved to find
Expression, she begins a melody,
So ravishing in sweetness, multitudes
Hearken enraptured—worship and applaud!
The universe is less to God than body
To soul—He infinite, the soul finite.
He actuates as certainly each part
As soul the body while it dwells therein.
Hence darkness is His frown and light His smile,
The tempests sweeping earth and sea His rod,
And gentle winds that softly fan the cheek
His loving touch, the hand to cheer and bless.
Old Paganism discerned the Deity
In everything, in nature everywhere
Traced agency divine, and peopled earth
And sea, the mountains, plains and groves with gods—
Religiously wiser and more devout

Than we, though they erred scientifically.
'Tis shame upon philosophy to give
The less and needlessly withhold the greater.
God is within development of all
And everything, and also is above
To guide in whole or part the universe—
Ubiquitous, supreme and infinite!
Each aspect of the myriad forms of nature,
His nature holy and divine reveals
And gives His own expression to pure spirit.
O! multiform and marvellous beyond
The thought of man or angel, e'en in earth
Endless variety in everything,—
In each we see the face of Deity,—
And all express the mind and thought of God!

Now we're content with gaudy toys,—but soon
Earth seemingly will slide beneath our feet
And vanish, leaving us in ether space
Alone in full view of the spirit worlds!
Then all the little thoughts and cares of life,
Our gold or honor, station or estate

Will seem as trivial as dust beneath
Our feet,—and longingly we'll yearn and cry
For thoughts befitting immortality,—
And seek to know the dwelling place of God,
And realize His near and loving hand
To guide us through the vale and shades of night!
Alone in light divine we see the light.
Alone to drink from fountains pure, which flow
From spirit source, will satisfy the soul.
Apart from God, created spirit droops
And mourns, and shorn of all its beauty roams
And writhes in agonies of conscious guilt,—
A star aflame beyond the realms of bliss,
The sport of chance, beyond the sweet restraints
Of moral law,—upon which to look e'en pales
The face of heaven's light and casts a gloom
Like death within the realms elysium!

Unspeakable the advantage, and renowned
Moses became, when always he discoursed
Upon God's presence personal: within
The veil Shekinah's glory manifest

Was seen: upon Sinai His lightnings fierce;
Thence too the thunders of His voice were heard
In words distinct and clear, which terrified
The multitudes. Then Moses stood to them
In place of God, because the people feared
To hear the voice which thundered from the mount.

    No clergyman his office properly
Administers who fails in this respect.
Alas! how many fail and preach a jargon,
Pronounce their *sibboleths*, and ventilate
A little science, less theology,
And strive to please the ear and tickle fancy
Into profane uproarious applause,
Or stifling flattery, effeminate.
'Tis called professional, a science, art,—
And such it really is—an art to slay
The soul with opiates, when wickedly
Deflected from its true, divine intent!
    O God! remove the cloud obscuring earth
And sea, that servants filling sacred desks,
May look beyond and far into the heights,—

Discern Thy glory and Thy wrath and power,
And realize the great and good intent
Of their commission to a sacred work !
O ! give them vision of the Cross, suffused
With Blood, and melt their hearts, and fire their tongues
To preach of Christ and Precious Blood alone !

    O Precious Blood ! whose price can purchase worlds
From wrath and sin, whose stream can cleanse the soul,
Can Heaven restore to blighted, darkened earth,
Can bring the highest bliss from ether realms,—
Subdue the ministers of evil, quench
The fires of Hell, and conscience stings restrain,—
O Heavens ! in mercy pour its flood, as rain
Copious, upon our parched and barren souls,—
That life may quick return, and graces grow,
Flourish and render beautiful our lives !
In front of Pilate's hall beneath a crown
Of thorns, the fountain issues—crimson tides
To shame, confuse, appal the guilty earth ;
On Calvary the Fount becomes an Ocean
Without a shore—which throbs the love of Heaven !

Thus service in the church in sombre shades
And dark and lowering clouds, or light appears!

The desert training Moses had, was deemed
Of Heaven as necessary as the course
Afforded him in Egypt's schools renowned.
The culture of the ministry with care
And diligence, the human element,
In modern times is liable to quench
And supersede the higher spiritual,
Through institutions set apart, endowed
Richly, establishments where danger lies
To foster clergy aristocracy:
Called schools of prophets, artlessly esteemed
Such in good faith,—whence 'tis thought incense sweet
Ascends hourly, propitiating Heaven,
Like that behind the veil upon the altar
Holy within the sacred tent—the prayers
Of saints, which render venerable and holy
The very ground where stand the monuments
Munificence and piety have built.
Such ought to be a fact pre-eminent!

Lo, Bethels! but endowed and rich—ambitious
And proud, they're corporations corpulent;
In danger imminent to pedagogue
The weak to worship them in servitude
Abject; and then, alas! they'll God dethrone
Where scientifically He's ably taught:
Then spirit power, apostatised, becomes
Parent prolific of gross ills, which quench
Humility, the lamp of holiness—
Her light obscured where most it needs to glow;—
And Heaven becomes o'ercast, and clouds draw near,
With lurid flames and thunder peals surcharged!

    Titles for patronage, most plethoric
Are in the church and schools and agencies,
And foster aristocracy and caste
Where most humility ought to prevail
And crown a sacred ministry, adorned
And honored most by love to God and man,—
Where parity is claimed, but least exists!
If Christ, our Lord, were titled Doctor, Pope
Or Cardinal, 'twould seem and be profane!
The Shepherd of the sheep, our Saviour meek,

The Pastor of the flock, is title quite
Enough for Him, and ought to satisfy
His servants too, who're called of Him to serve.
Had apostolic times addressed the four
Illustrious Divines, as, Doctor Paul
Or Peter, James or John, our ears would stand
Askew—we'd judge their hearing quite impaired.
Now schools inflict, and modest names are made
To glow like comets by the tail they sweep
Athwart the heavens;—and long as they are light,
Or rarified proportioned to their length,—
And too like consternation may create,
As comets do, of some disaster near!
    There is a spirit power in Agencies,
In seminaries, boards and colleges,
In churches, neighborhoods and families—
'Tis recognized by whate'er dominates;
Controlling, giving gait and character,—
As spirit dominates in man and gives
Complexion to whate'er he is and does—
Renders him angel-like in beauty, grace
And mien; or ugly, vile, repulsive like

The fiends in nethermost abyss of hell!
As man both thought and character impresses
Upon whate'er and all he has to do,—
So God or angels, good or bad, the soul
May rule. Hence Scriptures teach that man should
    pray,
And alway strive to have the Holy Ghost
His Helper—only safe and blessèd then!
When He the soul controls, His lineaments—
Most tender, loving, beautiful, are seen
In us in acts and words and character—
Heaven stooping to the earth, and man to God
Conformed in image, beauty and in thought,
As seal to wax impressed by hand divine.
Though Spirit Infinite all space pervades,
Each atom and the universe entire,
Yet spirit finite independent acts
At times, responsible, for thus it may,
Though living in a spirit atmosphere
Encircling all,—and it in Person God,—
Yet He, Supreme, in love may not control
Direct or indirect, for reasons best

Known to Himself, which finite mind in Heaven
May understand and fathom, but not here.
And ne'er against our will does He constrain.
Alas! we're often left to act alone,
To plume our wings and soar abroad without
The Parent's help, and ne'er from danger then
Are free.   In sinning we're unhelped of God,
Act wantonly and may destroy the soul!
If happiness our life adorns, our soul
Must exercise itself in things most pure,—
Must bask in heaven's atmosphere, where love
Supremely reigns without corroding wraths,—
Be strong and valiant for the truth and God:
And on the other hand must shun whate'er
Corrupts, degrades or renders gross the soul.
In either case 'tis spirit power enlarged,
Matured by what it feeds upon, for good
Or evil, for this and the future life.
The world is what the spirit in it is!
  Where'er an evil tendency exists,
'Tis more than martial glory won in arms
To fearlessly forewarn, denounce in love

That's true,—which has an air and grace angelic,—
Which neither begs nor fawns, palav'ring sweet
With words effeminate in elegance—
Base sycophancy; genuflected—slave
To power and tinsel popularity!

 'Tis true that many in the chairs of schools
For sacred learning are heaven's noblemen,
And so are very many whom they teach.
For such in quiet parishes to teach
And learn, and fast and pray,—or Christian life,
Humility and Spirit Power divine
In light and grace cause to pervade, control
And saturate, and thoroughly, with glow
Of love the sacred schools, this paramount
To precious lore there taught, would educate
A ministry to revolutionize
The times and bring millennial glory near;
And make the tongue aflame with eloquence,
Because of love intense for God and man,—
With ne'er a thought of introducing self
For honor, praise or gratulation vain;
And kindle in their place a heavenly light!

Man Redeemed.

Jesus! who left His throne, earth's Teacher great,
In solitudes His heavenly thoughts conveyed
To His disciples, chosen from the poor,
And hallowed every place, where sorrow's wail
Invoked the gracious help divine of Heaven.
He taught and loved as man has never done,
And left a legacy for future times
Of wisdom, grace and power to save the earth
From sin's sad blight, and disenthrall her sons
From Satan's power and give them realms of bliss!

Dear Lord! how sweet it were to sit beneath
Thy feet and have Thy ruby lips distil
The dew of heavenly wisdom in our soul
Enraptured, whether on the mountain peak,
In vales, upon the sea, or by the way;
How great the privilege vouchsafed to man
To journey at Thy side, endure the ills
Of poverty as though possessed of worlds;
To rest in hovels poor, or palaces,
Alike content with Thee in every place;
To see no good except with Thee, dear Lord!
To gather treasures of the heavenly realms

Of Thee, oh Saviour! every place alike
Is Heaven,—Thy presence renders nothing hard,
Nay! renders sweet what otherwise is ill!
    A mission holy sanctifies a place;
No place can sanctify a worldly heart.
Where'er the blessèd feet of Jesus trod,
Where'er He taught beneath the canopy
Of heaven, where'er He prayed in midnight hours,
Or rested by the way, 'twas holy ground.
The chairs of doctorates in synagogues,
And rich preferments in Jerusalem's
Great Temple, honors which the world bestows,
And multitudes with eyes distended wide
And open mouth pursue, He justly scorned.
His followers alike can bless the world,
And sanctify the place their feet abide,
However poor, howe'er distressed or lone,
And soon convert the world to Him, shed light
In every heart, if they'll His lesson heed—
In love with Him—His smiling radiance,
The beauty of their Lord, their highest joy—
His presence bliss—His service their delight,—
To serve as He has served our blighted earth!

Moses, a man of God illustrious,
And mighty both in words and deeds, drew nearer
To things invisible to human sense
And spirit world, than any man before
Or since his time. God's love his pious wish
Indulged while hid within a rocky cleft,
Displaying to him His similitude,
Restraining him the while from drawing near.
To see His face we'd die of love for God;
To see His glory there, would kindle flames
Within our breast which nature could not bear,
Insufferable, so bright and beautiful!
Hence are His features veiled from mortal sight,—
And Moses e'en was lovingly restrained
From looking in the face of Deity!
Though almost idolized, because so noble,
Erect in body, beautiful in soul,
Yet mortal, having flesh and bone, the time
Drew near that he must die, e'en while his strength
And force were unabated, and his sight
Undimmed. He died in Moab and was buried
There by the Lord Himself, who carefully

Concealed his sepulchre from mourning Israel,
And gave archangel Michael charge thereof,
As cherubim guarded the gates of Eden
To prevent a worse evil than the fall.
'Twas doubtless merciful, and heaven's intent
To save all Israel from idolatry,
The worshipping the dead or relics—called
Sacred and venerated by the Church
Of Rome, as Israel doubtless would have done.
But Satan claimed the right of tempting Israel,
As he'd before tried Job by grant of heaven.
Too often had His people Israel fallen
For God to trust them thus in Satan's hands.
Upon one occasion Joshua, the high
Priest, side by side with the angel of the Lord
Stood, and lo! there was Satan to resist,—
Whom sternly then at once the Lord rebuked.
Iniquity is bold, and Satan none
The less! Now Michael strong and pure pre-
    vails
Against the arrogant and subtle Tempter.
But Michael railed nor cursed, but mildly said,

The Lord rebuke thee, Satan. For pure spirits
To maledict would compromise themselves.
Michael did not refrain from using harsh
Words because impotent, or from a fear
Of law divine, but patience marvellous
And moderation characterized him
In that most notable, but not the only
Contest with the archfiend: example for all
And each of patience even with the bad.
For heaven even with the obdurate
And flagrantly corrupt is loving, mild
And tender, always using gentle speech
And moving words of sympathy and love,—
Except for hypocrites within the church,
The whited sepulchres of mere pretence
To piety and love for God and heaven.
Language fails to express for such heaven's scorn!
To maledict the hopelessly corrupt,
Without intent or possibility
Of doing good to them or others, betrays
A spirit like the maledicted angels.
If lost, 'tis fitting that we pity them,

In heart feel sorrow and inwardly weep,
E'en as o'er Jerusalem Jesus wept!

Michael with Satan fought to render heaven
Pure, and expelled him from the sacred place :
No contest otherwise in church or heaven.
The stream which most adorns to bless the world,
Is never dry like cisterns made by man,
Is always at its fountain head most pure,
Nor fearing in its source the summer droughts
Is God's beloved church, the greatest gift
Which heaven bestows upon the world and angels.
More than in aught else earth possesses, heaven's
Beatitudes and glory reappear
In her—its source and Head forever sweet
And fragrant, sparkling pure and lovable.
However pure the source, the stream by man,
In acts overt or by neglect of duty
Which God enjoins, may foul become, impure
To some extent, which carefully the saints,
Redeemed by blood Divine, and ministers,
Appointed watchmen in the church, should guard

With jealous care and great solicitude,—
And smile at laurels, gaudy, puerile toys
Which lure the vain, the wise degrade to fools,—
And only long for service worthy high
Ambition, to exalt the lowly, help
The poor and raise the race to eminence.

    Always the church has more to do with evils
And sins and tendencies thereto, within
Than those without. To rail, as many do,—
Making it a pastime professional—
A service cheap and easily performed,
Against the infidel, the flagrantly
Wicked, the sceptic, Satan and his angels
Is shooting at too long a range, and wastes
Missiles, the enemy not usually
Just then within their sight. They'd doubtless flee
In case he were. But it's the popular
Preaching, and safe for any seeking help
And commendation, patronal regard—
Whose fingers always feel the people's pulse.
Thus none are hurt, and evils in the church
Are winked at, and remain untouched and grow

Apace—whose pastors, false to sacred trust,
Are dormant, feasting while their churches die !—
And doubtless popular, of whom all men
Speak well,—but possibly too in accord
With flesh and world, against whom Christ pronounced
Solemnly woes,—for thus the prophets false,
Said He, were in regard. For Satan ne'er
Molests the faithless, fearful, politic
Divines, who covet more the praise of men,
Whom daily they commingle with and know,
Than fear the frown of heaven which they fail
To see. The clergy have to do with sin:
Enough they'll find within the church and heart
At hand—if not too fearful to institute
A search. To render pure the church redeems
The world, saves sinners, preaches gospel truth
In every land,—gives joy where sorrow reigns !

    Let men not fear to own the truth,—the fount,
The human heart is foul, and none's exempt.
All liable to err should watch themselves !
We've God alone the Fount of purity
For all that is, which live and move and think.

The streams the feet of sinning men and angels
Have rendered foul,—but all the while the Fount
Is pure and sweet, and sparkles ever bright!

    The last conflict will doubtless be with demons
In hearts professing zeal for God, deceived
Deceivers 'mong the saints, malignant foes
Of righteous men and enemies of truth,
Unholy men within the church—as Satan
With Michael when he strove for Moses' body—
Not infidelity and all without.
The world to harm the church is powerless
While Zion's sons are true and pure themselves.
And victory will ever crown the church,
Never uncertain, when in faith and prayer
She fights the sins that are within Herself,—
And trusts to God for victory o'er the world
And every form of unbelief without.

    Alas! that faith should not enlarge and glow
E'en here, by knowing, fearing, loving Thee,
O God! who art revealed so lovingly
And bright to earth and heaven, to man and angel!
With naked eye we never see, but souls

Discern in Thee, O God, an Ocean, o'er
Its lucid bosom e'er a calm, with ne'er
A ripple, ne'er divided into streams,
In essence One, in glory One and power
The same—yet never Father, Son, and Spirit
Holy have seemed eternally but One
Since worlds and spirits into Being came!
What countless lustres gleam and radiate
And glow in varied shades eternally
Therefrom, the heavens ne'er fully will reveal!
The Father reigns and dwells alone, in Him
The self-existent Son forever lives,
From Them the Holy Ghost, a Person each,
In deepest depths of love forever reign!
The Spirit Dove abides where Christ is loved!
The like is unrevealed, surpassing thought!
No shadow e'er obscures that intercourse,
That blissful life, that dreadful Trinity!
What power, finite, can cope with Infinite?
But wondrous love is Theirs, and wisdom just
As bright, and mercy to the sons of earth.
    We think of Thee beyond our little space—

And present too ; we think of Thee above,
Below, and near—and also hope, within !
Beneath Thy shade we lie ; the fleecy clouds
O'erhead we watch—nor fear their wraths the while !
A soft and glowing light their borders fringe,
And darkness is suffused with golden rays,
Which symbolize our lives and sorrows here,—
For God is light, whose beams illume our homes
And hearts and shrines, e'en when the darkness hides
Whate'er is bright and beautiful from view !
'Mid showers of tears love ne'er more sweetly beams,
Nor smiles more radiant glow, in trust and love.
In thought of Thee, our littleness we feel,
And tread with modesty earth's sacred paths,—
But conscious of Thy love, without a fear
Of Satan, man, or beast, or storms abroad !
The ills which from within beset our way
Are harder far to bear and overcome
Than like in others seen, or in the world.
When self is overcome, subdued and rests
In God, there's victory, a rout, triumph
Where battle must begin, to issue well !

Oh, God ! unveil Thy sweet face, Heaven illumed,
That we may know and fear and love Thee more,
And flee the sins which turn Thy face aside,
Thy beauteous face, or hide Thee from our view !
    Fidelity of spirit power appears
In lovely light when self is first subdued,
A harder task than fighting other men—
And more distasteful to a nature fallen.

    But Moses, though his body died, did not
As to his person sleep in the dark grave.
For person is not body which we see,—
Invisible forever it remains
Except so far as 'tis revealed by substance
Material, of earth or ether pure.
The person of the prophet had escaped
The soul's casket dead, for which Satan strove.
A body spiritual was doubtless given,
Of heavenly origin, of flesh and blood
Divested. And let us indulge the thought,
That chariot and horses all ablaze

With fire of dazzling beauty, heavenly,
Transported earth's chief prophet, loved of God,
Triumphant, up-borne, swift as tongues of flame.
The glowing wheels dashed o'er the firmament
From star to star, in seeming scorn of space
Which intervenes between the earth and Heaven.
Angels upon the battlements of heaven
Assembled, welcomed his approach with joy.
The city, ere gained, opened wide its gates,
To let the chariot triumphal enter.
With gladness seraphim and cherubim
Became escorts through heaven's streets to thrones
Where Jesus welcomed him, amid heaven's shouts,
And melody produced by angels' skill
On instruments tuned to heaven's harmony.

   No previous era brighter dawned and shone
In earthly splendor more than did the fifth;
Which engages now in brief space our thought.
   'Tis monarchy, high eminent in earth,
Enthroned, to see by grant of heaven what man
Can physically do, by using earth's

Best gifts, to render happiness and peace
Supreme, to conquer all the reigning powers
Of evil and afford security.
That man's a failure history records!
    This era dawned in David, and its bright
Meridian attained in Solomon,
And closed with monarchy enslaving Israel,
Depository of the church of God.
Repeated futile efforts monarchy
Made to regain its place and power and throne,—
Lost by arraying power against the church.
Imperial Rome the last enslavement made
And sadly closed this most eventful era;
She in turn broken, destroyed by Spirit Power:
The same as Pharaoh's kingdom and his throne,
And Babylon the great of lesser guilt.
A solemn truth the past and present teaches,—
That churches are destroyed whene'er in league
With carnal powers in every overthrow,
Like gold refined what's pure alone preserved;
Or when enslaved by them the powers themselves
Soon cease, expire and come to bloody end!—

But ne'er can be enslaved except untrue
And base and faithless to her solemn trust!

    Same truth again, appearing manifest,—
Disaster comes and eras end, when God's
Church lapses into sins which quench His Spirit.
This only revolutionizes earth
And man, and never fails in speedy change,
And judgment great or light gauged by the sins.
Hence earth gives signs of woe when churches fall—
And well she may, for judgment is at hand,—
E'en while the church is busily engaged
And exercised about the sins in others
And in the world, and everywhere except
Within herself: as did self-righteous Jews,
Who railed against, maligned and crucified
The Lord Himself! To introspect would harm
Entail upon none, but good alone convey;
But actual harm, or little good is done
By most prospecting telescopically.
In keeping with the common themes discoursed
Upon sins keenly searched for in the world,

Or hell, or ancient times, to moderate
Excuse or quiet pangs of conscious guilt,—
Not a few readily too often detect,
With seeming pleasure, sins in others, make
So fierce assaults upon them, you'd suppose
They'd set themselves to guard the lives of States,
Or that the world were all ablaze,—who least
Of any class, e'en by mistake will act
With common sense, intelligence, or wisely
Discern their own, and introspect themselves ;
Who more should fear the treachery of sin
And wrong and ills within their bosom nursed,
Than e'en malevolence in others' breasts !

 Many are those who wish and work us ill,
Like cruel wolves that howl afar for blood,—
For sin abounds—but grace much more, in hearts
Allied to God and saved through love Divine !
Jesus, the accusations priests alleged
In envy and in hate, He meekly bore,
And silent faced accusing multitudes.
Oh, blessèd Jesus ! Thou hast taught us how
Best to endure and conquer spleen and wraths,

Or scandals vile, malicious, evil speech,
Or accusations false,—by setting seals
Upon our lips, where words but feed the flame,—
By calm, angelic dignity—the mien
Of Heaven—too high to stoop to men inflamed
By demons, kindred spirits of their own,
Who're harbored, and to whom a willing ear
Is given seductive speech and harmful schemes!

    O come, let us each stand beneath the Cross,
And see ourself the guilty wretch who costs
The patient Saviour, groans and tears and blood!
Oh, Jesus! give us light which shines most clear
From Calvary's Cross, illume our guilty selves,
And break our hearts, and open founts of tears
From seeing sins within, from learning more
Of self, and hating sins that made Thee mourn
And die upon the tree which man matured!
Then service in the church a light will shed
The world will scarcely fail to recognize,—
Discerning purity to emulate!
The church from shade to light will then arise
And shine in beauty's Spirit Power, Divine!

The shrub that yields the sweetest flower has thorns,
The road that leads to eminence is rough,
And dark the night that yields to clearest day,—
So man is crucified to enter Heaven!—
But woe to them who perpetrate the crime!
Within the vales and quiet solitudes
Of earth may pleasures reign, but glory comes
In crowning radiance through suffering!

Since Israel asked a king, contemned the reign
Of heaven, the Lord ordained that man should see
The phases good and bad of monarchy,
In all its varied aspects:—man enthroned
Upon the earth to reign in Sovereignty;
And man enslaved by man in greed of power;
Man crueller than fiercest reptiles seen
Ages ago in earth's dark history;
Whole nations slaughtered, streams with blood o'er-
    flowed,
Human gore steaming soils of every land,
Corrupting air and bringing pestilence
So rank and dire the beasts and birds escape;

The groans of innocents, of maidens, babes
And aged sires, and writhing agonies
Rendered the themes for sportive glee, comment,
Hilarity, and O! discordance,—hell's
Malignant mirth excelled and made to blush
On earth by men—by kings enthroned in power!

  With David, faithful, true to pastorate
The ewes with young and guard with vigilance
The flocks committed to his care, this era
Begins in seeming promise of most blessed
Results. In Bethlehem secure, content
And happy 'mong its hills to range, where born;
And in its plains to meditate and sing
Along its tranquil rills the livelong day—
His life melodious with harp and song,
Without a thought or care for luxury
Aside from that enjoyed, which ministered
Then to his soul, the highest known in gift
Of heaven to man,—there Samuel, the great
Prophet of Israel unannounced appeared
At Jesse's feast and found the Shepherd boy;

Discerned, through Spirit Power, the qualities
In him of royalty, and there anointed
David with holy oil the future king
Of Israel; that with skill, integrity
And purity of heart the chosen people
Of God might be fed by a pastor's hand.

    Samuel, unhelped by Spirit Power; would not
Have chosen the rustic, who before him stood
Unsandled and unwashed, with naught about
His loins except his shepherd frock, with staff
And sling in hand, uncouth and innocent,
Without a thought beyond his father's flocks:
The beauty of his character, his power
And worth, were by the seer yet undiscerned.
    A lesson here is given that all may learn.
The modern church her pastors choose—a trust
Freighted with good or ill in spirit life.
Alas! if lacking piety and grace,
Committees, deacons, elders magnify
Their office and judge captiously the force,
The depth, the orthodoxy and the logic

Of candidates—weighed in their balances—
Whether too they have wealth or titled sires;
And aged matrons over spectacles
Look sharp, and eye their manner, tone and gait—
Their office to detect and note each flaw,
And learn if they're of children innocent;
While maidens gay, both young and old, discuss
Their smiles, complexion, figure, and the cloth
They wear, the set of their cravats, the kind
Of perfumes used, and whether young and sweet!—
If candidates for matrimony too—
A mormon priest would scarcely fail a call,—
Then are of Spirit Power Divine such churches
Bereft, unhelped of God and carnally
Inclined, and look as Samuel did at first
Upon Eliab, ere God announced His choice.
But churches seeking Spirit Power and help
Divine, in faith and prayer, which pastors choose
Who're able to instruct, and wise to lead
A flock in pastures green, along the stream
Of life, and bring them safely to the fold
Upon the plains of Eden, are blessed indeed!

The spirit power of churches alternates
Between both good and evil, light and shade,
Where light and good alone should sweetly reign—
Sole atmosphere where reigns the Holy Ghost.
Blesséd indwelling Spirit, Comforter
Divine, alas ! that any should restrain
Thy power and glory which relieves the Curse,—
To bear their pains and griefs without Thy help,
Without Thy healing touch to soothe their ills,
To calm their fears and dry their tearful eyes !

    A blesséd gift to Israel,—but for David,
Sad, inauspicious was the day when taken
From sheepcotes and his native hills and vales
To occupy a throne and wield a sceptre.
His solitary, happy, gleeful life
And innocent peace bid adieu forever !
    Great was his power to win the hearts of men,
Developed in after years when called to rule :
With ruddy face ; clear open countenance ;
Comely, but goodly person ; with eyes bright
And fair and mild,—but flames when passions kindled

In his breast through wrongs done himself or others;
Swift as a wild gazelle upon mountain crags;
With strength of arm to break a bow of steel;
Agility to leap a wall, as wild
Deer scorn a hedge which intercepts their path;
And courage to assail a lion and bear,
Moved by a bleating lamb within their jaws,
Or giant from Philistia defying
Israel, and slew the lion and bear, and bore
Away the giant's head and sword in triumph,
Qualities winning and admired by all.
Though rival, Jonathan loved more the son
Of Jesse than man does a lovely maid,
Caring not though supplanted in the throne;
The virgins too of Israel, songs of praise
With harp and timbrel sang to him, the prince
With every manly quality to win
Or conquer every heart with ease and grace;
And Judah jealously, with love intense,
Watched o'er the youngest son of Jesse, claiming
Him their own darling prince, of their own tribe
Born to high destiny, as they discerned,

And tremulously watched his steps, pursued
Upon the mountains like a partridge wild,
Through forests, wildernesses, and in caves
By envious Saul, jealous of his power.

    Thus disciplined he rose superior
To every foe, became imperial,
A conqueror, whom none successfully
Withstood, the Lion of Judah and of Israel.
His prudence and sagacity in war
And peace were ever manifest ; along
With simple trust in God, childlike, devout
Dependence on Divine and Spirit help.
Seldom such qualities combine in one :
But combined nothing surer than success.
A sterling character and marvellous
David was, combining opposite traits
In harmony,—with passion, tenderness ;
With fierceness, generosity enthroned
In sweet munificence within his breast ;
A soldier and statesman equally great ;
His hands red with blood, yet a shepherd king,
Whose wanderings and wars and sufferings

Better instruct our race than the after reign,
Magnificent, of Solomon, the son ;
Often betrayed he fell into gross sin,
But just as quickly heaven's throne in tears
He sought, and always fought for mastery
O'er all that was impure in human hearts.
He illustrates in truth the poverty
Of poor, fallen human nature's best powers
To overcome the tendency of all
And each to sin, and its impotency
To reinstate itself in holiness.

 Thus more than any man before his time
He was a type and prophecy of Jesus
Of Nazareth, and antedated Him
One era, the ancestor of Messiah.
And David was His likeness, portraiture
As near as sinful human nature can
Portray the Lord, Divine, a Sufferer!
Was prophet, priest and king, and shepherd dearly
Beloved ; who left his native hills and home
Upon the call of heaven, his peaceful life
Abandoning, foregoing happiness,

To pastorate God's flock with jealous care.
He raised a throne illustrious throughout
The earth, a legacy of zeal and love
To Solomon, his youngest son, who ate
The fruits, enjoyed the luxury, his father
David had purchased dearly with groans, tears
And blood throughout his most eventful life.

 Hence Solomon's reign becomes typical
Of what our Lord has purchased for the world,
Redeemed and saved by tears and blood divine:
But no more fully typifies this truth
Than sinful David does the Lord of glory.
The after glory follows the Messiah
As Solomon was type ideally
Of glory heaven will reveal to saints
When each a daughter, decked in Heaven's jewels
And crowned with diadems, will sit upon thrones
In heaven's New Jerusalem, redeemed!

 The House of God, the church in purity,
Alone of earth is man's asylum tranquil,
A refuge from the tempests, wrecks and deaths

In earth! We drop our sandals at the door—
The place is holy—reverently bow
The head uncovered in the sacred shrine.
Though not a burning mount with thunders fierce,
But peaceful, still as conscience cleansed of guilt,
Yet fervent reverence the worshippers
Becomes, for holy is the Lord presiding,
Above the heavens venerable, Majestic!
Earth trains, but perfects neither saint elect
Nor church: hence neither finds a home on earth—
But do in fields elysian in the heavens!
The seen and natural reveal to earth
And man a spiritual house, unseen
Save by the spirit power inhering in
The soul, revealed as vast and glorious,
A spiritual universe to come,
Imperishable,—happiness without
Alloy, advanced above the present state
Beyond compare, to reign forever then,—
Of which the present church is emblematic,
Or like the husk enfolding grain with care
Till ready for the harvest, reaped by angels.

The chief foundation-stone in Zion laid,
Precious, elect is Christ the world's great King;
After whose image every stone is fashioned;
Whose virtue energizes and pervades
The whole, by Spirit Power adorned for heaven.
The reign of Solomon best typifies
The church millennial, known through prophecy,
When Zion's daughters will awake the harp
And lyre to sing the glory of the Lamb
With melody more marvellous than earth
Has ever known; when sons redeemed by blood
And agony which Calvary reveal,
Will reign as prophets, priests and kings in earth,
Magnificent, excelling Solomon.

  Thus man with measured tread and steadily
Is ever nearing blissful homes beyond
The skies. Though pilgrim here and hard the road
Each hour adorns and beautifies the soul
For heavenly courts, not far removed, ecstatic.
The darkness, sorrow, pain and deaths of earth
In contrast render heaven sweeter far
And beautiful beyond what angels know.

Born to the purple, Solomon was cradled
In luxuries and had a peaceful reign.
Of noble presence, he adorned a throne
And held the sceptre gracefully, and reigned
With fascination, idolized by nations.
The fairest son of earth maternal,—face
Ruddy, and locks dark mixed with golden threads,
With eyes like dove's, and countenance as bright
As Lebanon and excellent as cedars,
The chief among ten thousand, perfectly
And altogether lovely—cherished prince
Adored and madly loved by tender queens;
Who won the daughters of Jerusalem
And every heart throughout his royal realm.
Above this beauty physical were charms
Of spirit gifts and power so marvellous,
The casket of the soul, the body's charms
Were lost to view, eclipsed by brilliancy
Of intellectual force; of wisdom far
Reaching, minute and accurate, and skilled
To range the universe or humble realms
Where plants and beasts teach men of Spirit Power;

Of ready sympathies with sufferers—.
A noble spirit quality in princes ;
Of genial humor, playful, giving life
And charm to every place his presence filled—
Society with him a luxury
Rarely vouchsafed to men in gloomy earth !
Thus dawned the splendid reign of Solomon.

    The world as far as known contributed
Its choicest treasures to Jerusalem
Which then became a vast emporium
For riches,—gold of Ophir so lavished,
That servants in the court of Solomon
Glittered therewith in coats of mail and shields,
Their hair too powdered daily with its dust ;
And silver like the stones that paved the streets ;
Cedars from Lebanon like sycamore
Trees in the vales ; and Tyrian purple lavished
Upon princes of the imperial household.
Truly the golden reign of Solomon
In grandeur was colossal, ravishing,
And great and rich in all earth's luxuries.
His vessels navigated every sea,

Exacting contributions from all lands
To render him earth's most glorious prince :
Of Ophir gold, of Sheba precious stones,
Spices and perfumes from Arabia,
While India and Ceylon furnished trees
And flow'ring plants, both beautiful and rare,
And animals, and birds of plumage rich
For parks and sylvan vales, which Solomon
Planted and nursed for his luxurious
Abandonment to all the sweets of love
With female beauties, glittering about
His steps whichever way he turned, with grace
And blandishments, each one displaying charms
Possessed by each, and jealous of his smile.
His palaces excelled whate'er in earth
Had been effected by the hand of man
Before or since his time : upon Lebanon,
High eminent for prospect, cool retreat,
And in Jerusalem with ivory
And cedar, and adorned with silver, gold
And gems, he built without regard to cost
And lavishly his habitations, marvels

Of beauty, grandeur, elegance and taste.
A Paradise to rival ancient Eden
He planted too at Etham with rare trees
And tropic fruits and flowers and fragrant herbs
Of varied scent, and gathered there both male
And female singers, rendering the air
So redolent with sweets that heaven seemed
To have resumed her reign once more in earth!

  His glorious sovereignty was world renowned.
Fair Queen of Sheba in the far-off south
Moved by his fame for wisdom, love and wealth,
Journeyed in state befitting queens, with trains
Of camels bearing gold and spice and gems,
To Palestine to see and hear the prince.
The calendar contained no brighter day
For Solomon than that when Sheba's Queen
Arrived and was received in grand triumph
By all Jerusalem and Palestine.
She seated at his side upon his throne
Of ivory and gold, arrayed before
Her was the splendor of his court and state,
His wealth and lavish prodigality

Upon his servants, messengers and maids—
Each one a noble prince or princess seemed :
And spake to her of nature animate,
Inanimate, of life and character :
Communed with her upon the universe,
The world, their glories and their mysteries :
And let us hope, upon redeeming grace.
Seeing and hearing all the Queen's heart sank
In admiration, and beneath the splendor,
The wisdom and the beauty of the prince,
Confessing that the half had not been told
Her by her courtiers in her princely halls ;
That servants at the feet of Solomon,
Seeing his face, receiving from his lips
Wisdom distilled like early morning dew,
Were happier, more blessed, than reigning kings.
    How different the Son of God esteemed
All earthly wisdom and this kingly pomp,
Who in the after era judged it less
And not to be compared in beauty, grace
Or sweetness with the lily of the field,
Modest and unpretending in its worth,

Hidden, but none the less to be esteemed—
Indeed the more if shrinking from display.

    When Solomon began his reign he seemed
Devout and zealous for the God of Israel;
And built a Temple seemingly a gift
Of heaven to Jerusalem,—so grand
And beautiful that mortal sense confused
Was dumb and blind beneath its dazzling wealth.
He prayed for wisdom, not for holiness
Also; alas! that simply he might rule.
Hence passion for the glory and renown
Of earth absorbed his noble powers and quenched
The better qualities which marked his youth,
And doubtless grieved the Spirit Power, Supreme,—
Selfish became, conceited, arrogant
And proud—terrible self idolatry!
The golden era then began to wane,
And unresisting Solomon allowed
His heathen wives to build and sacrifice
In temples dedicated to their gods,
And introduce in Israel heathen rites.

    Known evils once allowed ne'er of themselves

Die out, or loose their hold in earth or hell,
But grow, accelerated and increased
In power and virulence by length of years,
Unless subdued by good and faithful men,
Or if the church lack grace, by Spirit Power.

    The Moloch worship introduced became
In after years an awful blight to Israel.
Young men and helpless babes were sacrificed
With maidens to the Cretan Monster, vile
E'en as an image with bull's head and horns
And body like the human; Israelites
E'en, prompted by their love of gain and fear
Of reigning powers and kings—a potent force
Working death in all times—engaged in rites
Both cruel and atrocious, causing sons
And daughters to deliver up themselves
To death, to pass through fire,—and shed the blood
Of innocents—were deaf to pleading babes,
To piteous hands and cries in vain addressed
To adamantine hearts,—who were parents once,—
But now bereft of feeling rendered fiends!

Depraved, none know themselves, the human heart,
How foul and venomous it may become,
How despicable, wicked,—an abyss
Whose reigning passions, like a liquid fire,
May burn and rage till every good impulse
And noble sentiment of innocence
And purity, so sweet in childhood days,
Will be consumed and vanish like the mist,—
For evil stronger—impotent for good,—
An angel babyhood which ravishes
A mother's heart because so passing sweet,
Matured into Satanic lineaments!
None realize what crimes they'll cheerfully
Perpetrate, lest restrained and helped of heaven;
What monsters they'll become, mature in guilt;
Make evil angels weep or skulk away
In solitudes, repenting of their work!

  Upon a grander scale a church corrupt,
Allied to flesh and world the following
Era—apostates foul of hell let loose—
Practised the most refined barbarities;

And slaughtered hecatombs of human saints;
And plotted 'gainst a remnant pure in heart,
Whose blood beneath God's altar ever cries
For judgment yet reserved for cruel men,
Now chained in hell, reserved for awful fate!
    And so may any church at any time
Become corrupt, then cruel, e'en the church
Called Protestant, if evils are allowed
To grow, and ministers fear to rebuke,
Or study ease and popularity,—
And churches estimate their worth thereby,
Inquiring not as to fidelity!
    Earth is a battle-field where right will win,
Though saints lose heart when God Himself seems hid,
When enemies abound, when victory
Seems theirs, when vile and godless men bear rule.
That God's beyond the reason's height, beyond
Our thoughts and fears, too often we forget.
But faith in God ne'er loses heart, nor hope
Nor courage,—e'en in darkest hours will strike
For victory, the issue leave to God,
And dare to side with what is pure or right,—

Which scorns the praise of men, the world, its wealt.
And luxury, if Jesus leads the way !
Hence back into the field of strife we'll go,—
With God, for God, to bravely do our part,
Nor falter in the ranks, where saints may fall—
They lose but earth and win a royal crown !
For this is God's command to every saint.
A calm obedience is sweeter far,
And loyalty more dear than sacrifice :
For sacrifice may measured be, but love
Is measureless and hungers more when fed,
And feeding, more enjoys the heavenly feast.

 When evils reign and wrathful men afflict,
Oh ! hear the music voice that ne'er deceives,
And see the tender eyes all moist with love—
A beacon light upon a stormy sea
To guide us safely home to Heaven and bliss.
'Tis Jesus, tender Shepherd, hunting lost
And silly ones, who've scattered from the fold
Because of wolves which render hideous
The night with howls—and feared though they're
  afar !

The world is bright and fair and beautiful,
The woods, the flowers, the bubbling rivulets,—
But man is treacherous and cruel, false
And vile, and renders dangerous our way,
Entangles us in snares, afflicts and gloats
O'er miseries produced by hellish arts!
Ah! then a voice from Heaven, as zephyrs soft,
Enchants our ears, fresh courage gives, a light
Imparts like pearly morning's struggling rays
Which dawns upon eternal, heavenly day!
Our tears are dried, our fears give place to hope,
Our lamentations, cries and wails to smiles!
Now light grows brighter, flashing from the Throne,
And fears of hell, and minions coursing earth
And sea therefrom, take flight like shades of night
Before the flaming coursers of the Sun!
Divinely sweet and glad, the heart then rests
In God and God in it, nor fears nor sees,
Oblivious, the wraths of earth or hell!

    Thus spirit power in cruel persecutions
Is seen, and dark, or lurid red with blood,—
In moans of agony outdoing earth's

Liquid fires or the Ocean's fiercest storms :
In contrast light appears in power where faith
Abides and lovingly reclines in God !

    Not solely Moloch's cruel rites of worship
Did Solomon permit and foist upon Israel :
For also then commenced the worship lewd
And shameful, too abhorrent for detail,
Of Ashtareth, the Hieropolis
Goddess of Syria—most popular,—
For human nature fallen loves whate'er
In church or world is most intensely human,
Though shocking low, lewd, debased and foul.
Legend tells us the goddess Ashtareth
For ten years in Tyre lived a prostitute.
Hence maidens beautiful and young in years,
And women to her in unchastity
Consecrated themselves as acts of worship,
In temples too and built to her for lust,
Religion, so called, used to cloak their crimes.
Such were the rites and others sacred called—
Rendered to devils, which great Solomon

Allowed his wives from foreign lands to graft
Upon Israel's worship pure, ordained of heaven.
 A dreadful warning, loud and easily learned,
Against whate'er corrupts to be allowed,
Though seemingly a trifle, in the church.
'Tis here that Satan and his sons begin
Attack and quench the light in human hearts.
Thus great was Solomon's fall from the heights
Of glory, ne'er attained by sinful man
Before, into idolatry and depths
Of sin involving nations in his guilt!
And thus he proved, as David had before,
Humanity and sinful frailty.

 'Tis right the church should rule in earth by love,
Rebuke with tenderness, a haughty throne
Assail, defend the poor and suffering,—
As David seized a lamb from cruel jaws.
For thus her moral light illumes the heart,
And glorious her reign, excelling kings,
Whose splendor pales, is insignificant
Compared with hers which sheds a mellow light.

If true to missionate our fallen race
And cheer with light the hovels of the poor—
Which never fails in rich returns for labor,
We'll then upon her face prismatic hues
Of holy light discern, and she'll fulfil
Her office, first in order :—ne'er to render
Herself a thing to be despised by man.
Apostatized she is apostemate !
If arrogant, inflated, self-content
The curtain falls, and gloom and night hang o'er
Her future, totally her lineaments,
So fair in light, concealing from the world:
'Tis then dense shades assume the place of light !

    As man was made by special act of heaven,
By Spirit Power, the sixth creative day,
So Christ assumed our flesh and bone the sixth
Era of the redemptive period,
Which now we've reached in progress of the theme.
At evening's hour, God said, Let there be light,
As in the eras past when each began !
Developments and then decadences

Are seen in eras of the period
As in creative days.   If each were called
A day, no damage done.   Our era ends
When churches fall, when Satan rules in hearts
Professing love to God and in the church,
As in each era of the past as seen,
Like Israel lapsed into idolatry.

    Our era with the Saviour of our race
Began, who layed aside His robes of glory,
For so decreed, and took upon Himself
The form of man to suffer in his stead.
In plants and flowers and all material things
The sun's light is reflected, else our eyes
Would fail their office in the dazzling rays :
So in the Son, God's image glorious,
The true Jedid-jah, well beloved of God,
Of melting, overpow'ring lustre shines.
Indeed an ocean of light floods all space,
And beauty new, reflected from the throne
Of God, when thus is lifted the dark veil
From Spirit Power, majestic, filling earth
And heaven and the universe entire !

In Bethlehem, incarnate Deity
Was born a babe divinely sweet and fair,—
Whose name is precious, and refreshing more
The soul in every age than aught of earth.
The Saviour's advent God's eternal love
Displayed,—a light to beam within the soul.
Of purity immaculate Himself,
Yet He our sins assumed and bore their curse.
The sacrifice of victims, unresolved
Through ages, reached its goal, resolved in Him
The victim, slain for sin, though Heaven's Son,
The Lamb of Calvary while earth gave signs
Of woe in terror and in sympathy,—
While men, for whom the sacrifice was made,
Were instruments or else insensible.
Unparalleled, unspeakable display
Of love divine and power to vanquish hell !
Christ was the true Shĕlômôh, prince of peace,
A prophet, priest and king ; in spirit filling
Immensity ; as Saviour of the world
Assumed humanity and suffered death !
    He bridged the mighty gulf and paved the way

Which men e'er since in long procession trace
To the sublime and heavenly abode.
Our fathers dear and friends have trod the path
Which we, when death shall come, shall also tread.
Escorted by the angels we'll from earth
Hasten our steps above to higher birth—
Our spirit-form ethereal like the sky,
For all that's earthy shall the earth absorb.
The way's illumed through all the trackless gloom
By yonder sphere of bliss whose golden light
Bathes brightly all the way from earth to Heaven.
The beaming Fountain is the Throne of God
Whence springs the light to guide through sorrow's dark
And thorny road to pleasure's endless day.
Oh! then with heavenly glory crowned we'll see,
Embrace and weep the tears of glad delight
Upon the bosoms pure, once loved below,
Of parents, wife or children gone before—
But thrilled by joy and love beyond degree
By seeing Jesus crowned, once crucified!
   Malignant spirit burst with violence
In storms of deadly wrath against His person.

But when with lamb-like patience Christ endured
And bore malignancy, hell ne'er before
So felt its impotency.   Love subdues,
Where hate and opposition stir the fires
Of evil, gratifies the powers of earth
And hell,—and sinful man's alike inclined.

   This era in millennium attains
Its acme ; its decadence in the reign
Of Satan, when unbound he'll range the earth,
Be given liberty to tempt the race
As ne'er before.   But only when the church
Becomes corrupt and falls, submiss to him,
Guilty of sins exceeding other eras,
Will earth be burned and utterly consumed,
As in Lot's time were Sodom and Gomorrah,—
A prophecy of what's reserved for earth !

   Each thoughtfu. pilgrim through this vale of light
And shade in earth, from infancy to death,
Is often perplexed in seeing multitudes
Without apparent thought of God or Heaven
Or Hell, of blood and bone to us akin,

And who in earth are prosperous, have wealth
And luxury and ease and elegance;
Some revelling in sins and wickedness
Without restraint or punishment divine,
Shocking a spirit keen and delicate!
While lovely is the world, yet sin prevails,
And ills and trials darken many a home!
Apparent only is the mystery.
Wherever sin prevails the heart is dark,
Because the Spirit light Divine's withheld:
Wherever Zion's graces meekly reign
There's light and joy and peace akin to Heaven,—
As 'twas in Egypt night, while Israel sang
Sweet songs of praise beneath the shining sun.
Where God abides, makes manifest His power
In love there's light that gladdens every heart;
Where He withholds His loving Self, the realms
Are dark, and men are suffered to disport
Themselves and revel in the sinks of vile
Impurities, and stain their hands with blood,
Inaugurate the reign of Hell at will—
Without the living God without restraint!

For men, inclined to sin become as beasts—
And worse, without the Spirit Power, Supreme,
To lovingly restrain and guide the soul,
Co-act and bless and dwell therein,—in type
Prefigured by the Blessèd Trinity!
In union with the Living God there's life,—
Especially to souls so heavenly blessed.
Communities where such abide have peace :—
And men who're there and covetous of gain
Are helped, not hindered to amass their wealth,
And here enjoy unconsciously the light
And gifts and peace of Heaven—their only Heaven!
Alone! dissevered,—souls adrift and left
To act their own perverted thoughts and wills,
Like wand'ring stars and comets glow with light
Baneful, portend and bring a reign of blood,
Confusion, fear and death—where God is not !—
So far as known, to manifest His grace!

  Eternity is short by half for praise;—
Infinity is short by half for place
And altar for the worship due our God
If union does subsist betwixt us both,—

And He's our Guide through all this wilderness,—
Our Dove who hovers o'er our heads to bless,—
Our Father waiting in the heavenly courts,
Expectant upon our steps, and waiting long,
As though impatient to embrace His own—
Enfold us in His cloud of light and grace,
As Moses was upon Sinai's holy mount,
To cause to glow with beauty all divine
Our every feature of the soul and face
And body spiritual, of ether pure ;
And give beatitudes, to those akin
Enjoyed by Father, Son, and Holy Ghost !

The seventh era was revealed to John,
A Sabbath rest, when earth and heaven, new
And saved from fire, will glorious appear,—
Our Sabbath of the period a type,
Recurring every week and teaching man,
That rest, a holy, blissful rest is near ;
When darkness, sorrow, pain and sin are o'er ;
When all the shades, obscuring moral light
And quenching joy, shall never more appear !

Then shall the church in glory shine, complete,
Symmetrical before a universe,
A star alone in ether, beauteous,
Upon nothing hung, twinkling in amber light,
The most adored of all the hosts of heaven.
Each son and daughter perfect, glorious,
Emitting heavenly light, ethereal,
Among whom and where God shall dwell and reign
More manifest in beauty and in power
Than earth or stars or Heaven hath yet revealed!

    Within the barren isle of Patmos lone,
The agéd prophet sat disconsolate;
No sound of kindred voice to lull his soul,
Harassed and suff'ring wrongs for witnessing
For Jesus and the truth; all still save winds
From the Ægean Sea which breathed their soothing
    notes
Within his soul. There suddenly, while wrapt
In thought and mourning o'er earth's wickedness,
The last seer given to the world saw gates
Celestial open wide, and then appear
Visions so glorious, that, o'erpowered

By heaven's splendor, he became as dead!
The New Jerusalem, the Holy City
Adorned, his spirit saw: whose splendid light
Was crystal clear like jasper stone; whose walls
Were great and high, and placed at each pearl gate
An angel guard; and the foundation walls
Garnished compact with precious stones and pearls;
The streets like glass transparent, paved with gold.
And voices, with ten thousand harps, were heard
Commingling harmony with shouts of praise.
The glory of the Lamb they sang, His works
Marvellous and His judgments manifest.
One multitudinous voice like the roar
Of thunder or of waters many, sang
With love the praise of God, omnipotent.
The symphony of voice and harp, the praise
Of Heaven, no tongue can speak. The prophet mute,
Awe-stricken, paralyzed, was dumb with fear!
The saints redeemed he saw in shining ranks
By myriads; clothed in linen white; washed clean •
By blood divine, saved from pollution's stain
By Gilead's balm,—who, joined by seraphs bright,

Sang too the praise and glory of the Lamb
Slain—song more rapturous than that which angels
Gave when earth first appeared among the stars.

  There from beneath the throne he saw a river
Issue like crystal clear, which o'er rich beds
Of amber, luminous stones, gems and gold
Flowed through this Paradise of God. The meads
On either side with roses damasked, tinged
Like Sharon's and with many a varied shade;
And lilies, which there flourished blushing meek,
Immortal; there the palm, the cedar grander
Far than on Lebanon's mount, and the olive,
More beautiful all than in Eden grew.
The citron there full-grown with foliage green,
On whose full boughs hung golden luscious fruit
Of pleasant taste, reviving sight and smell.
There grew the tree of life on either side
The river, transplanted from Eden's plains,
Whose fruit the blessed may eat—the angels' food—
And drink of the waters pure. Beneath this shade
Refreshing, o'er the diamond sands and paths
Of burnished gold, the blessed redeemed may walk,

Accompanied by their Lord, whose countenance beams
With love intense upon His precious flock
Which gather at His feet to hear His words,—
As erst in Galilee when journeying
To bear the Cross and suffer Calvary!

    The Saints how beautiful they are, how bright
In bliss their glories shine: but brighter far
In beauty is the Lord! compared their light
Is dim and paled, or totally eclipsed!
No marvel saints have died of love for Him;
Have borne imprisonment and torture, fire
And sword for Him; His beauty broken hearts
When once He's been seen all aglow with light!
Pure saints how happy in their love of God,
Their hearts kindled into a brilliant flame—
Sweet unction—by his excellence alone,
When seen or felt—loved for His own dear Self!

    May we indulge the happy thought, that God
Permitted Satan man to tempt and sin
To enter Eden that He might effect

A greater good, subdue the Powers of darkness,
Show Spirit Glory in a manner new
To heaven, and save and raise our fallen race
To eminence ; that man upon a throne
Might sit, be crowned with Heaven's diadems—
Above the angels, who ere man was born
Were made and entered Heaven ; sublimer good,
Both manifold and wondrous in extent,
In human nature honored, dignified,
And now invested with divinity !
Thus man in truth redeemed is upon a throne,
With emerald light encircled nighest heaven's
Great King !   The mystery of creature sin
Through Spirit Power evolves thus partially
And pleasantly, promoting thought or love
To God and Heaven and every creature made.
For sin is incidental to a good
Through love and mercy ; God revealed in light
Which ne'er before beamed from beneath the veil !
Thus Job was tempted by permit of Heaven,
Covered with boils by Satan's agency,
His property destroyed and children slain :

And unadvisedly he spake at times ;—
But ultimately was exalted higher,
Made richer, happier, more prosperous
And blessed of God above his former state,
To such degree, the former was almost
Forgotten and eclipsed by heaven's bounty.

    In light and shade is Spirit Power revealed:
'Gainst darkest clouds the purest light is seen :
Without the shade the light is less discerned.
Yet 'tis the province of the meanest souls
To struggle always for the purest light ;
To be within the glow of light Divine ;
To think and do naught bringing shade and night
Upon, within the soul—remorse begun !

    Ne'er will eternal years divinity
Exhaust,—for there's always some new display
Of God's deep, fathomless immensity,
Of spirit pure and infinite, above,
And yet pervading all and every thing !
The possibilities of Spirit Power
Are only faintly seen below the skies

By what already perfect has been done:
By marvels, beautiful and gorgeous, like
The wings of butterflies from crawling worms.
For Spirit Infinite the elements
Willèd into Being, and the chaos spoke
Into light, beauty, wealth material
So marvellous throughout the universe,
And beauteous in plants and beasts and birds—
Too multiform, complex for mind to grasp,
And varied infinitely—ravishing
With joy the heart of spirit lovable!
He too our souls, felicitous can cause
To sparkle in variety and scope
Endless and marvellous. By what He's done
A prophecy of what is yet to come,
For earth material and spirit life!

Hark! songs angelic swell o'er earth and sea:
How sweet, oh, blessèd sweet! the strains that tell
Of life anew, and sin and sorrow o'er,
Of shadows fled, of death and night all past!
Oh, how their echoes sweetly ring from crag

And mountain top, o'er hills and through earth's vales :
For rest has come at length,—the day has dawned,
The beauteous day which prophecy foretells,—
In welcome home at last at journey's end
Upon the breast of life's untroubled sea.
Sweet songs—but from above a chorus rings
From angel lips aglow with bliss and love,
Where multitudes are hovering o'er and near
Man blessed, redeemed, and Paradise restored!

 Transporting glimpse of home, the heritage
Of angels and of man redeemed, who'll be
Whate'er they think and know and feel and hope ;
With power commensurate with will, where Christ
Bears rule and holds the keys of life or death.
So erst His blessèd feet to calm repose
Thrilled stormy Galilee's tempestuous sea,
While wond'ring marines beheld themselves
Transported to the shore without the aid
Of hands, at once as through the air—all space
Annulled—all fears allayed and hopes fulfilled.

 The home beyond, the soft blue shore across
The stream, the narrow stream dividing death

And life, how near at hand it often seems,
Within our vision, nay, beneath our feet,
While wistful hearts look o'er and long for rest,
Release from pain that dims the sight for earth!
When dreary, dull and dark our present home,
Often then sunbeams aslant to earth seem ways
Inviting, shining paths which lead to Thee—
Oh, Heaven! oh, fragrant shore with flowers of bliss,
Into the golden light beyond the sea!
Oh, sweetest thought! within that home to lean
Upon the breast of Jesus evermore!
Alone! within some unfamiliar place,
And strangers lost, without the right to walk
The royal realms, and trembling pale with fear
We'd be without the blessèd Jesus there,
To wait and watch and welcome us within;
And teach us how to lisp in angel tongues;
Endure, enjoy the sights ne'er seen before,
The fragrance heavenly, taintless pure and sweet;
To bask in angel loves forevermore!

    Ah, then! far off, below will lie the sea,
The earth a star, a gloomy star appear,

Veiled as in shades, in shadows dimly seen,—
While in the splendors of the beams of Heaven
We'll walk, or upon the orbed and golden clouds
Without, above the City's jewelled shrines,
Look out upon a universe beyond!

    My God! is this the exchange for sickness, pain
And death, anxiety and earth and woe?
O chariot! to bear us into realms
Of bliss, thy wheels delay their coming long,
While notes astray from Heaven reach us here,
And beams from Zion's gates ajar are seen!
And all unmerited, a gift of grace,—
The price of blood Divine, of Calvary!

FINIS.

www.ingramcontent.com/pod-product-compliance
Lightning Source LLC
Chambersburg PA
CBHW030746230426
43667CB00007B/856